LAUNCHED TO ETERNITY

LAUNCHED TO ETERNITY

Crime and Punishment 1700 - 1900

Glyn Parry

The National Library of Wales
2001

Cover illustration: woodcut of an execution accompanying *The Confessions and Behaviour of Henry James and Catherine Griffiths Executed for Burglary October 7. 1791.*

ISBN: 186225 030 8

Designed & Printed by Cambrian Printers 01970 627111

INTRODUCTION

Crimes and criminals have always fascinated and terrified us. Millions of us watch television programmes like Crimewatch with its reconstructions of crimes, documentaries showing how particular crimes were solved, documentaries about the recruitment and training of police officers, and fictional programmes about crime and the police from Dixon of Dock Green in the 1960s to The Bill in the twenty first century.

Tabloid newspapers provide exhaustive details about sensational crimes and criminal trials, usually crimes involving violence such as murder, armed robbery and burglaries. None of this is new. Nineteenth century newspapers provided even more details of particularly horrific crimes including word for word transcripts of evidence in criminal trials and lengthy descriptions of executions. Going further back to the eighteenth century, news about terrible murders and robberies was conveyed by ballads. Since the majority of people were illiterate two hundred and fifty years ago, ballads were meant to be sung in public - usually on fairs and market days - so that they reached a far wider audience than simply the literate. Ballads were afterwards sold to those who could read them.

The practice of singing ballads about the most sensational crimes continued in Wales until the late nineteenth century. To draw attention to his tale the ballad singer carried a long pole decked with a red flag. Around his neck he would carry a placard showing life-size pictures of bloodstained murder weapons. Since 1700 then, the media may have changed, but the message has not. We are still as fascinated today by crime and criminals as our ancestors were three hundred years ago.

CRIMINALS

MURDERERS

Like today most victims of murders in eighteenth and nineteenth century Britain knew their murders very well (the notable exception to this was murder committed during a

Part of a broadsheet depicting the murder of Gwenllian Lewis by her husband entitled in translation *A Lamentable Song in Memory of the murder of Gwenllian Lewis...by her husband Joseph Lewis, July 1857.*

robbery that will be discussed later on). Murders and victims were often members of the same family or near neighbours with a long history of bitter strife and quarrels. Murders committed within the family reveal a picture of quarrels, physical abuse and finally the breakdown of marriages, or they reveal parents seemingly unable to cope with bringing up their children.

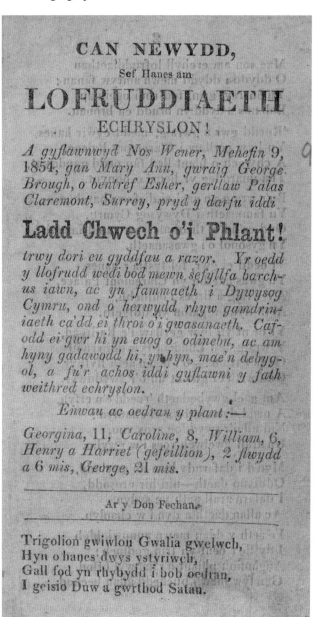

Ballad about the murder by Mary Ann Brough of her six children, 1845. A respectable woman, she had been a wet nurse to the Prince of Wales.

The courts keenly sought evidence of quarrels and marital breakdown in cases of murder within the family in order to discover whether the murder was deliberate or not. Thus Rees John was suspected of murdering his wife by slitting her throat in Neath in 1760 only because he had often threatened her and physically ill-treated her which eventually led to their separation four years before the murder. William Griffith (of whom more later) was executed in Anglesey in 1830 for attempting to murder his wife after years of bitter quarrels followed by separation.

Mountgomdy ss. The Exaiacōn of David Rees and Edward William both of the pish
of Pennegoes in the s'd County yeoud taken before us Sr Charles Loyd
Barrt and Morgan Edwards Esqr two of his matyes Justices of the
Peace for the s'd County the thirteenth day of January Anno D'ni
1720 as ffolloweth

The s'd Exaionts upon Oath depose and say that on Munday the ninth day of
January Inst'd Theese Depon'ts both for their livelihood and maintenance working
at the Mines at and nere A Towne called Dolcow and the s'd Lands adjacent
thereto vac'd: Dolcow'll Ward and out of Subslt and nere ffitt to their
P'm'aisōn they went both downe into s'd Pitt w'th desigue to gett up some of
the wood and timber made vse of therein when they by the light
of A Candle they theise Depon'ts tooke downe along w'th them for the
discoury of the wood theise Depon'ts when downe in the s'd Pitt
diswoud the Corps of one Catherine David ats Loyd who w'th her two
Children had been missing abt: fraue weekes before the s'd s'd Catherine
as first p'tiend comeing into that neighbourhood to the House of one John ffranis
of Dunquin in the pish of Pennegoes aforesd that at the time theise Depon'ts
went downe into the s'd Pitt one John Jones A smith by trade was staying
nere unto the s'd Pitt as he was allsoe when theise Depon'ts came out againe
after their discoury of the Corps aforesd: that before the s'd Edward William
who was behind (the s'd David Rees being got nere unto the top of the
s'd Pitt) called to him the s'd David Rees in Welsh and told him the s'd
David Rees that he was afraid the villain (meaning the s'd John Jones
was gone In ans'd whereto the s'd Jn'o Jones Expressd himself thus to the s'd
David Rees save my life, save my life, I have been here today before you
w'th Candle and fire: and at the same time ffurther Expressd himself to this
Effect that the Devill and her the s'd Catherine w'd have had him the s'd
Jn'o Jones to have throwen her the s'd Catherine downe into the s'd Pitt
and Imediately after sayd that he was w'in A Dozen yards of them

Robert Griffith of Connah's Quay in Flintshire was suspected and charged with the murder of his wife Lucy by striking her on the head with a pair of iron tongs. The only evidence for this suspicion was that as he was going to work on that fateful day Lucy was heard to say that she wished her husband would 'rot in the roof' and not return home if he was going out to work. This was taken to be evidence of hatred between husband and wife and therefore that the murder was deliberate. Similarly, Lewis Cynfyn of Crickhowell was charged with strangling his wife in 1755 only because neighbours had heard them 'scolding one another' and because his wife had declared in front of over twenty witnesses that she needed a candle one night because 'One does not know where such a villain may meet me in the Dark and knock me on the Head', referring of course to her husband. When Lewis touched his wife's corpse, one witness stated that 'the Blood started out of the Nose of the deceased very strong upon his [the prisoner] touching her', a reference to the old and widespread belief that a murdered body would bleed when touched by the killer.

Husbands - but rarely wives - also murdered their spouse because of an illicit love affair. Two very notorious murders in eighteenth century Wales, which received widespread publicity, were the result of love affairs by men with someone other than their partners. The first involved John

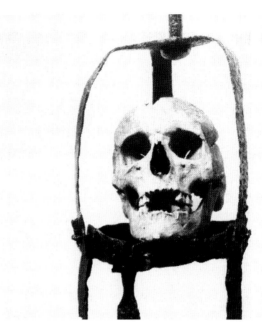

Photograph of the skull allegedly of John the Blacksmith.
By permission of The Museum of Welsh Life, St. Fagan.

Jones or Siôn Y Gof (John the Blacksmith). A native of Ystumtuen, Ceredigion, he left his partner Catherine David (otherwise Lloyd) there with her two children, Thomas and Avarina, whilst he crossed over to Montgomeryshire to

An exact Representation of the cruel Murder of William Powell. Esqr

N°1. William Spiggott. — 2. William Powell, Esquire.
3. David Llewellin. — 4. William Williams. —
5. David Morgan. 6 William Morris — 7. Morgan James.

Contemporary drawing of the murder of William Powell, Glanareth, esquire, 1769.
NLW MS 23206D, p.2.

Carmarthenshire — to wit — An Inquisition indented taken for our sovereign Lord the King at the parish of Pencarreg in the County of Carmarthen the sixteenth day of June in the tenth year of the Reign of our sovereign Lord George the fourth by the Grace of God of the united King of Great Britain and Ireland King Defender of the faith Before Daniel Price Esquire one of the Coroners of our said Lord the King for the said County on view of the body of Hannah Davies then and there lying dead upon the oath of David Williams, Timothy Davies Felindreyssa Timothy Davies Henday John Jeremy Timothy Davies Felindreucha John Biggs, Evan Davies, Thomas Williams, David Jones Pengelan David Jones Fanylan John James, William Williams and Rees Rees Good and lawful men of the said duly chosen and who being then and there duly sworn and charged to inquire for our said Lord the King when where how and after what manner the said the said Hannah Davies came to her death do upon their oath say That David Evans late of the parish of Llanfihangelrhosycorn in the County aforesaid Labourer not having the fear of God before his Eyes but moved and seduced by the instigation of the Devil on the thirteenth day of June in the year aforesaid with force and arms at the parish of Pencarreg aforesaid in the County aforesaid in and upon the said Hannah Davies in the peace of God of our said Lord the King then and there being feloniously wilfully and of his malice forethought did make an assault And that the said David Evans with a certain hatching hatchet made of Iron and Steel of the value of one — shilling which he the said David Evans then and there had and held in his right hand her the said Hannah Davies in and upon the right side of the neck of her the said Hannah Davies then and there divers times feloniously wilfully and of his malice forethought did hit and strike and that the said David Evans with the hatching hatchet aforesaid did then and there give to her the said Hannah Davies in and upon the right side of the neck of her the said Hannah Davies two mortal wounds each of the said mortal wounds being of the length of five Inches and of the depth of three Inches of which said mortal wounds she the said Hannah Davies then and there instantly died and so the Jurors aforesaid upon their oath aforesaid do say that the said David Evans her the said Hannah Davies in manner and by the means aforesaid feloniously wilfully and of his malice forethought did kill and murder against the peace of our said Lord the King his Crown and dignity And that after the said David Evans had done and committed the felony and Murder aforesaid he the said David Evans withdrew and fled for the same — And that the said David Evans at the time of the doing and Committing of the felony and Murder aforesaid or at any time since had no goods or Chattels lands or Tenements within the said County or Elsewhere to the knowledge of the said Jurors In Witness whereof as well the said Coroner as the Jurors aforesaid have to this Inquisition set their hands and Seals on the day and year and at the place above mentioned.

Coroner's inquest on the body of Hannah Davies, 1829.
NLW, Court of Great Sessions Records 4/766/4/31.

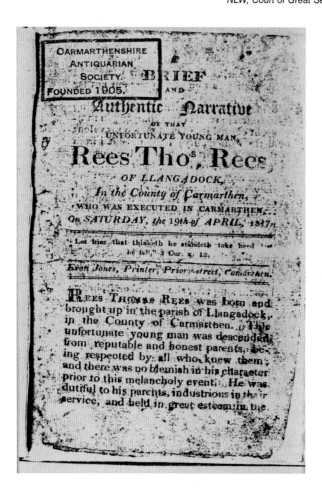

work in the lead mines at Dylife in 1720. Weeks later she went with her children to the lead mines to see how he was getting on. Unbeknown to her, however, John Jones had been having an affair with a local servant maid. Catherine, satisfied that John was fine, left for home after a few days. John escorted them for a mile or two; neither Catherine nor the children were ever seen alive again. Some eleven weeks later, miners, including John Jones himself, discovered the three bodies in a disused mine shaft which was being reopened. John had callously thrown them down the shaft. He fled, and tried to drown himself. His fellow miners ensured that he failed in his attempt to evade justice. He was duly tried, convicted, sentenced to death and his body ordered to be hung in chains near the place where the murders took place. According to tradition, he was forced to build the iron frame in which his body was to be hung. He was of course quite capable of doing this since he was a blacksmith. In 1938 a skull still inside what was left of the frame was discovered near where John Jones was allegedly executed: it is now in the Museum of Welsh Life in St. Fagan.

The second notorious case was the so-called Glanareth murder in Carmarthenshire in 1770 when a dozen men were charged with either the murder, or aiding and abetting the murder, of William Powell of Glanareth, esquire, a murder 'not to be paralleled in the history of Great Britain'. He had been stabbed twelve times, his nose cut off and one of his

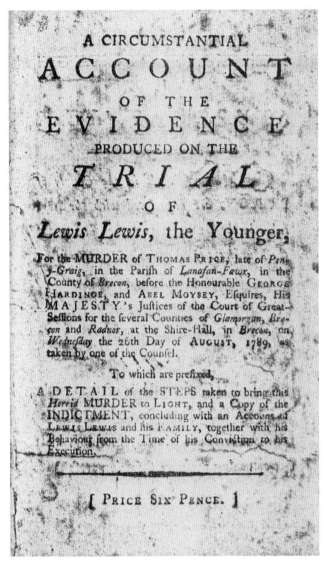

fingers cut through to the bone, by men who entered his house with their faces blackened with burnt cork. The instigator of the murder was William Williams, a draper from Llandovery, who had persuaded or bribed his confederates to come to Glanareth to serve a writ upon William Powell. It was rumoured, however, that Catherine Powell was having an affair with William Williams and that was the real reason for the murder. She was certainly separated from her husband and had been seen with William Williams in Hereford where she lived. Six were eventually executed for this murder.

Even in cases of murder involving members outside a family, the murderer and victim often knew each other very well. Many such murders resulted from unwanted pregnancies and often were botched attempts to induce an abortion with fatal consequence for both the mother and the unborn child. William Berwick of Montgomery tried to induce his girlfriend to abort by poisoning her with yellow arsenic. She died. Unwanted pregnancies led to two of the most publicised murder cases in nineteenth century Wales.

Rees Thomas Rees, a lay preacher, had made his girl friend Elizabeth Jones pregnant. Her parents refused their consent for her to marry because she was too young (she was 19). Faced with an unwanted pregnancy, no possibility of marriage, and the shame such a pregnancy would bring to both families, Thomas persuaded Elizabeth to drink a 'mixture of grey liquid...to purge her blood', probably to induce an abortion. Elizabeth miscarried eleven days later and died. Thomas was hanged in 1817.

The other case involved David Evans who deserted Hannah Davies when he found she was pregnant. When she tried to persuade him to marry her, as he had promised, he brutally murdered her with fourteen hatchet blows to the head. He was hanged (though not without incident as we shall see) in Carmarthen in 1829.

Other similar cases included the strangulation of his girl friend by Evan Jenkins of Llanwnnog in 1764 when he learnt she was pregnant. The banns of their marriage had already been published, but Jenkins was a very unwilling husband to be. He had sworn 'a hundred times that he would rot in iron before he would marry Elizabeth Evans.' John Evans murdered Elizabeth Williams because she was pregnant in 1825.

The other kind of premeditated murder was that resulting from long lasting disputes between neighbours. The most notorious example of this in eighteenth century Wales involved the Lewis family of Llanafan Fawr, Breconshire, and their neighbours the Price family. A bitter dispute existed between the families over stray sheep and, more importantly, over the Price family's belief that members of the Lewis family had been stealing their sheep for years. Matters finally came to a head in 1784 when Lewis Lewis the younger garrotted Thomas Price and threw his body into a pond and then proceeded to strangle his dog for good measure. Seven months later Lewis's brother Thomas saw the corpse floating about a foot under the water. Lewis and his father and namesake hurriedly put the bones in a bag, burnt them and scattered the ashes in their garden. Justice eventually caught up with them. Lewis Lewis the younger was executed and his body ordered to be delivered to the surgeons to be dissected. His father was hanged for inciting his son to murder. His brother Thomas saved his own neck by turning King's evidence against his own father and brother. The executions, not surprisingly, did nothing to end this bitter quarrel in Llanafan Fawr.

Almost forty years later, in 1826, another Lewis Lewis murdered a John Price in almost exactly the same spot. Local tradition maintains that the murderer was a grandson of Lewis Lewis the elder, and that the John Price was the grandson of Thomas Price. This seems unlikely. This case is one of the few early nineteenth century Welsh murder cases that produced a map showing the location of the murder.

Other cases involved a grudge. Henry Tremble, butler on the Dolaucothi estate, murdered his employer, Judge John Johnes, in 1876 because the Judge did not grant him a tenancy of an inn called the Dolaucothi Arms when it became vacant. Tremble had set his heart on obtaining the lease, especially after Judge Johns had half promised it to him. John Bellingham, a bankrupt and probably insane, held a grudge against the government, and became the only man in British history to assassinate a British prime minister.

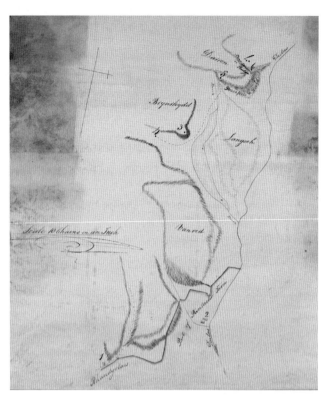
Map showing where John Price was murdered in 1826.
NLW, Court of Great Sessions Records 4/397/6/20.

Despite this catalogue of violent deaths, the overwhelming majority of murders were the result not of malice nor of intent, but rather of quarrels, fights or accidents. Quarrels which resulted in deaths were often occasioned by drink and were often caused by the most trivial of arguments: whose turn was it to buy drinks; the ownership of a walking stick; the right to graze sheep; bets; who was the strongest. Richard Jones was returning from working in the fields with his workmate Richard Gardner in 1826. A quarrel ensued over who was the best mower. Jones struck Gardner with a scythe which 'was stuck fast in the side of his face'. In 1764 John Probert the younger killed John Price in a fight in an inn because Price was blocking the fire. In cases of deaths after a fight it was crucial for the defendant to prove that he and his victim had been good friends, that there was no history of enmity or malice between them. A good example is the case of Edward Rogers who was charged with the murder of Mary Griffith, widow, in 1751 by shooting her in the head in an inn in Llandrinio, Montgonmeryshire. Numerous witnesses testified that there was no ill feeling between them and that they had 'been drinking each other's health and taking snuff from each other's boxes'. In many such cases the accused were either acquitted or convicted of manslaughter, that is, of killing without intent. This was the verdict returned on the parents of Sarah Jacob, 'the Welsh Fasting Girl'. They claimed that she had lived for two years without food or drink. People flocked to see her upon payment of a fee.

Part of Charlotte Johnes' entry in her diary describing the murder of her father by Henry Tremble in 1876.
NLW, Dolaucothi V 26.

6

Prison photographs of Sarah Jacob's parents, 1869.
Carmarthenshire Archives Service, ACC 2096.
By permission of Carmarthenshire Archives Service.

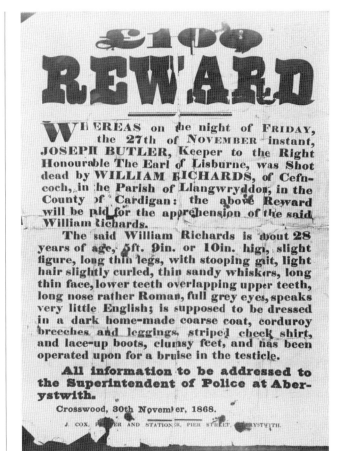

Reward poster for the apprehension of William Richards (Wil Cefn Coch) for the murder of Joseph Butler, 1868.
NLW POS27/13.

When a doctor eventually examined her she died aged 12 in 1869. Her father was sentenced to 12 months hard labour, her mother to 6 months.

Other fatalities were caused quite by accident. A bizarre accident occurred in the parish of Llywel in Breconshire on 30 March 1730. Elizabeth Roberts was distributing money to the poor of Llywel on that day. Unfortunately, all the money had been shared out by the time Janetta Rees arrived carrying - for some reason - a chamber pot. She lost her temper and tried to hit Elizabeth with the chamber pot, she missed and struck Mary Powell in the head instead. Mary subsequently died.

Not all murders were viewed with same horror. In some particular instances the people had some sympathy with the murderer. This was the case with the murder of Shadrach Lewis who was despised as an informer and blackleg. There was also some sympathy with those who had killed gamekeepers whilst out poaching. The most famous example of this in Wales was the case of William Richards (Wil Cefn Coch) who shot Joseph Butler, gamekeeper to the Earl of Lisburne in 1868. Despite the offer of £100 reward no one was tempted to betray him. On the contrary, local people hid him in barns, haystacks and in a mill wheel. On one occasion a friend even hid him in his wife's bed who according to the story was about to give birth. Eventually Wil was smuggled to Liverpool and thence to America. He reached Ohio in the spring of 1869 and was joined two years later by his girl friend. He died in the United States in 1921.

HIGHWAY ROBBERS AND FOOTPADS

Robbery, defined as stealing with violence, or threatening violence, was one of the most widely feared criminal offences. One of the main reasons for this fear was the fact that many robberies ended in murders. It was this fact which caused such great alarm, even though robberies formed a very small proportion of total crimes committed.

Robbers were separated into two groups, highway robbers and footpads - the equivalent of modern day muggers - who were widely believed to be more violent than the highway robber. Highway robbers, in contrast, were thought to be masked gentlemen on horseback who engaged in polite conversation with their victims before robbing them and then returning some of the money back. They were also believed to use phrases like 'Stand and deliver.' Much of this is myth. In only one case of highway robbery in Wales between 1730 and 1830 is there evidence of a highway robber acting like a gentleman. In 1741 Jane Harry was robbed by two men with their faces blackened. The robbers, according to her own testimony, robbed her of £17-19-0 (£17-80) and then returned six pence (2½p) to drink their health. This gentlemanly act did the robbers no good, however, one was hanged but the other fled before he could be arrested. It is unlikely that highway robbers in Wales actually said 'Stand and deliver' either. For one thing most of the victims could not understand English. There is one

Indictment for a highway robbery which includes the actual Welsh words used by the robbers, followed by an English translation, 1755.
NLW, Court of Great Sessions Records 4/617/2/23.

example in the court records recording the actual words used by a highwayman. The words spoken by one of the robbers was far more menacing than 'Stand and deliver'. He said in Welsh: 'Sefwch. God Dammoch chi efe ceisiwch arian chi' which the court translated as 'Stand God damn you I want your money.' This attempted robbery turned out to be a complete farce. The victims simply refused to hand over their money; the robbers fled but they were eventually captured and sentenced to seven years transportation.

Robbery by footpads could often lead to violence, especially if the victims showed the least signs of resistance. Violence was often used no matter what the victim did. Thus Sarah Thelwall was going to a 'dancing party' in 1825 with her friend Samuel Smith when they were assaulted in a Wrexham street by several men who stole her cloak. A year later in the same town Henry Bankes was quietly urinating against a wall when he was knocked down and robbed of five shillings (25p). But what received most attention from both newspapers and ballads were robberies that resulted in the victim being murdered. Ballads were published about Lewis Owen who shot his victim when he resisted his

attempt to rob him in 1822; about John O'Connor who robbed and attempted to murder two overseers of the poor, about Thomas Thomas who murdered a carrier from Silian, Ceredigion, in 1845; and about John Roberts who murdered school teacher Jesse Roberts before stealing his watch in 1853.

The case that received most attention, from newspapers at least was the so-called Dafen murder. In 1887 Thomas Davies, a clerk in the Dafen tin works near Llanelli, cashed a cheque in the local bank for £590 to pay the workmen's wages. On his way from the bank he was attacked by David Rees who struck him on the head with a piece of iron and murdered him. The murder caused a considerable outcry and the newspapers carried extensive reports of the murder and of Rees's trial and execution in 1888.

The cheque cashed by Thomas Davies minutes before his murder by David Rees.
Carmarthen Archives Service, Mus 411a.
By permission of Carmarthenshire Archives Service

A depiction of the murder of Jesse Roberts by John Roberts, 1853 and of the latter's execution from a broadsheet entitled in translation *A Lament on the Murder of Jesse Roberts*. The execution, especially, bears no relation to reality. This woodcut was used in a publication about Dick Turpin's execution over a century earlier.

A poem in Welsh written by David Rees to his mother shortly before his execution.
Carmarthenshire Archives Service, Mus 411a.
By permission of Carmarthenshire Archives Service.

Memorandum of
David Rees Your Son   March 17th 1888

My dear Father and Mother and Brothers
sister and relations all at penygar yspitty
Llwynendy Pontarllulgis Aberven and everybody
at Llanelly and all my friends.
I ~~do with you all goodby~~ goodby for ever and
ever my^a the Lord be with you Amen.

Dear Father & Mother Aunt Nance Unkle David
at penygar I am very sorry about you because they
are trying to put the fault on you about the money
but never mind those men that are trying to put
the fault on you they are nothing but wicked
men the same as those men that as sead what
~~as been sead about~~ ^me ~~and against me.~~

But I hope that you will forgive them the same
the same as I do forgive those men that as sead
those wicked things against me, And I hope
that you will pray and ask the Lord to strengthen
you to forgive them the same as I have had done.

May the Lord be with you
Amen

Letter from David Rees to his family on the day before his execution.
Carmarthenshire Archives Service, Mus 411a.
By permission of Carmarthenshire Archives Service.

BURGLARS

Burglary was as much feared as robbery and burglars could expect little sympathy from the courts. What people in Wales feared the most, and what gained most notice in the newspapers, was a confrontation at night with armed gangs of professional burglars. In Wales it was widely believed that burglars crossed from England to Wales or from the industrial towns to the countryside in order to burgle homes or to steal. There is in fact little evidence for this among the records of the courts. Only one case matches this belief between 1730 and 1830. Arthur Bennett, a wealthy man from Llandyrnog, Denbighshire, woke up to find his house being burgled by three men from Southwark, Surrey, armed with four pistols, a cutlass and an axe. One of the gang wore

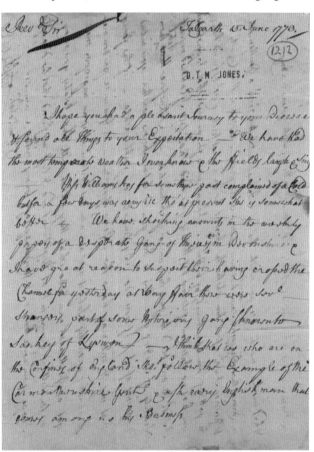

Letter from John Price, Talgarth, Breconshire, to Rev. John Jones, 15 June 1773, complaining about a gang of Devonshire thieves at Hay and suggesting that they adopt the example of Carmarthenshire gentry and ask every Englishman his business in the county.
NLW, D T M Jones 1212.

a mask resembling an old woman's face. Two of the men stole £30 worth of silver plate whilst the other stood guard over Arthur Bennett and his household staff. There were far more professional gangs of thieves and pickpockets who crossed over from England than there were burglars. Examples of these include 'Cockney Bill' and his 15 travellers who stole in Caerphilly and a gang of pickpockets from the city of Bath who were caught in Newport in 1842. So widespread was this belief in English gangs of thieves and pickpockets in Carmarthenshire in the 1770s that the justices of the peace there made it a matter of policy to ask everyone who spoke English in the county what he was doing there.

A belief in armed, professional gangs of burglars who made their living solely from crime also seems to be a myth. Most burglaries committed between 1730 and 1830 in Wales were committed by local men on their own. However there are a few examples of notorious burglars who burgled houses at every opportunity. Henry James of Eglwysilan, Glamorganshire, and his partner in crime Catherine Griffith of St. Fagans, were executed for burglary near Cardiff in 1791. Their confessions reveal a catalogue of burglaries in South Wales and England between 1789 and 1791.

Catching even one member of such gangs was often enough to break them up since, in order to save his own neck, a member would often turn King's evidence. For example, a gang of four Swansea burglars were apprehended in 1826 on suspicion of burgling a house in Oystermouth. One of their members turned King's evidence; the other three were tried, convicted and sentenced to death. Two of the gang were first suspected of burglary because when they were examined their bodies had been severely scratched in their attempt to get rid of the blacking, which they had used to disguise themselves.

Disguises were rare. A female burglar named Sophie James from Wiston in Pembrokeshire burgled a house dressed as a man. Despite the disguise she was caught, convicted and transported for life. Armed burglars were also rare. It appears that those who were armed, usually with swords, were former soldiers such as Thomas Jenkins of Llangyndeyrn, Carmarthenshire, and his accomplice William Griffith. Both were executed in 1789. Confrontations with armed gangs of burglars were also uncommon in Wales because burglaries were not usually discovered until the occupants of the house had woken up in the morning. However, the householder's nightmare, a confrontation with an armed gang in the middle of the night, did occur occasionally. The following is an (abridged)

Prison photograph of a Carmarthenshire burglar, 1864.
Carmarthenshire Archives Service, ACC 2096.
By permission of Carmarthenshire Archives Service.

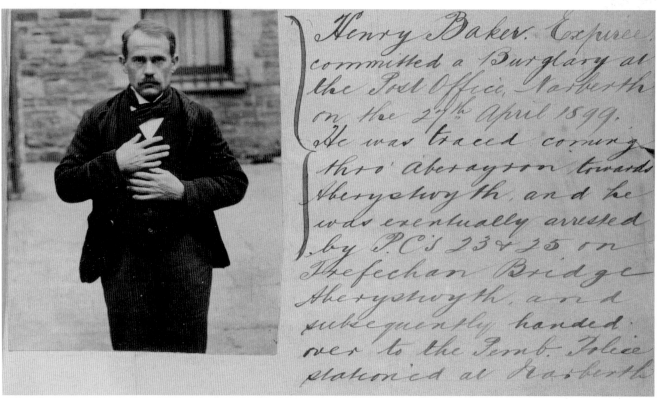

Aberystwyth police photograph of a burglar named Henry Baker, 1899.
NLW MS 23203B, f.9.

October 4, 1791.

HENRY JAMES alſo ſaith, that to the beſt of his belief, he is about twenty-five years of age, was born in the pariſh of Eglwſylan, in this county, of honeſt and induſtrious parents, and that there never was the leaſt imputation upon his character till he became acquainted with Catharine Griffiths; but that ſince that unhappy connexion, he had given himſelf up to idleneſs and bad company, and was acceſſary in all the robberies which Catharine has confeſſed ſhe had committed with him; was privy, aiding and aſſiſting to them, viz.——

The robbery at Roſs, for which he was tried and acquitted.

The robbery of the Laundry on the Norwich road.

The robbery of the Waſhhouſe, near London.

The robbery at the Summer-Houſe, belonging to his Royal Highneſs the Duke of Cumberland.

The robbery in Herefordſhire, at the houſe where Catharine and Sarah were ſo hoſpitably treated.

The robbery at the houſe between the New Paſſage and Briſtol.

The robbery at Old Sodbury in Gloceſterſhire.

The robbery at her Grace the Ducheſs of Beaufort's, at Stoke, in Gloceſterſhire.

The robbery at the Summer-Houſe of Thomas Edwards, Eſq. at Landaff.

The robbery at Landilo in Carmarthenſhire.

The robbery at St. Nicholas in Glamorganſhire.

The robbery at Sully in Glamorganſhire.

The robbery at Knole in Gloceſterſhire.

The burglary at the Stables of St. Pier.

The burglary at the Stables of Tredegar.

The burglary at Gabalva. And

The burglary at Park.

Serial burglar. The undetected crimes of Henry James from *The Confessions and Behaviour of Henry James and Catharine Griffiths Executed for Burglary October 7. 1791...*

account of such a burglary by the victim in Pembrokeshire probably in the mid 1830s. It conveys an atmosphere of fear, threat and menace:

I heard my wife making a melancholy noise. I saw the desk open and the prisoner standing close by the desk & a candle lighting in the desk by powder [and the prisoner] walking to the middle of the floor with a sword in his hand and a soldier jacket, black mask on his face and a cap on his head with a black fringe round the bill trimmed with red on the top. I hallowed so much as I could to awake the girls. He told, `No noise or else'. He said, ' I am a Robber & I got sixty men at my

command and I decide to call them in'. And my wife told me to take the candle from the powder or else it would blow the house up. I took the candle and put it on the table. Prisoner told, 'Deliver the keys and all your Money.' My wife begged on him to spare us our lives and he should have the whole. I brought the keys to the table. He ordered the money. I brought a purse with £8-14s and he ordered more and I brought him a purse with £29 and he ordered more. I brought him all my silver and he put the whole in his pockets and he ordered drink and my wife went to the cupboard and gave him a tumbler of gin and he ordered more money and I brought £75 of notes in bills and I opened them. In that time my wife went out of the room and he did look at the bills and gave a push to them. The sword was in his hand practising constant close to my head and I told him I must dress. I found it very cold

Before then he cried out and after, `My name is Rubroi [Rob Roy] the Chief of Robbers. I have robbed England, France and Scotchlan & now I come to Wales. I have heard that people got great deal of money in Wales', and he asked me to tell him who had money that he might rob them, but I refused. He told me: `Tis death for me to break in to your house and tis death for you. The judge is coming very soon to Haverfordwest & a very severe judge he is'.

My daughter came down stairs and asked me for her mother & I told her that she was up stairs & and she told `No', and he asked her had she some person with her. She told him `No', and she went up stairs in search for her mother. And he asked me for something to drink...& I went to the cellar to fetch drink to him and he followed me and I gave him the drink & then he wanted to see my wife. And my daughter was crying about her mother & I told him she must be fainted or his men had killed her. And he wanted to kiss my daughter & I told him that I would risk my life before he should touch my daughter.

Only a minority of crimes involved violence. There were far more cases of petty thefts and drunkenness than there were of murders, robberies and burglars. Among the more unusual convictions recorded is one from Merioneth reproduced on the following page.

TO CATCH A THIEF

One of the most important features of criminal detection in the eighteenth century, and indeed well into the nineteenth century in some places was the lack of a professional police force to pursue and apprehend criminals. Victims of crime had to do any required detective work themselves, though friends and neighbours would also assist sometimes. Even when a suspect had been caught, it was the victim of the crime who had to prosecute and to pay costs, though from the 1750s the State would repay costs in some successful prosecutions. Little wonder then that victims of crime simply did not bother to pursue suspects or prosecute thieves, especially if the stolen goods were of little value,

County of Merioneth to wit.

Be it remembered, That on the *30th* day of *August* in the year of our Lord One Thousand Eight Hundred and *seventy two* at the Justice Room, in Corwen, in the County of Merioneth, *John Day* is convicted before the undersigned, *two* of Her Majesty's Justices of the Peace for the said County, for that he the said *John Day* on the *22nd* day of *August* 18*72* at the Parish of *Llandrillo* in the County of *Merioneth* unlawfully did on and by the side of a certain public Highway called the *Tynywern* Highway there situate and in a certain exposed situation near thereto and within a certain distance of the Turnpike Road called the Corwen and Bala Turnpike Road there situate ~~out~~ ~~of~~ cut up and deposit the Body of a certain Beast to wit a Camel

contrary to the form of the Statute in such case made and provided. And we adjudge the said *John Day* for h*is* said Offence to forfeit and pay the Sum of *Five Shillings* to be paid and applied according to Law, and also to pay to *Thomas Hughes* the *Informer* the Sum of *One pound nineteen shillings* for h*is* Costs in this behalf; and if the said several Sums be not paid forthwith

we adjudge the said *John Day* to be imprisoned in the Common Gaol at Dolgelley, in the said County, and there to be kept to hard labor for the space of *fourteen days* unless the said several Sums and the Costs and Charges of conveying the said *John Day* to the said Common Gaol, shall be sooner paid.

Given under *our* Hands and Seal*s*, the day and year first above-mentioned, at *Corwen* in the County aforesaid.

An unusual conviction.
Merioneth Record Office ZQS/490/25(M).
By permission of Merioneth Record Office.

14

because it simply was not worth the trouble and expense. David Jones, a farmer from Radnorshire, spoke for many when, after catching a burglar red handed and striking him several times with a whalebone whip, declared that he would rather give a 'few stripes than go to the expense of prosecuting'. Because victims of crimes were unwilling to try and apprehend suspects or to prosecute them when they were caught, vast numbers of criminals were never brought before the courts. This - the so-called 'dark figure of crime' - may have been as high as 90% of all crimes committed.

So how were those criminals that were prosecuted in the courts apprehended in the absence of a professional police force? In certain types of crime, such as thefts from the dwelling house, it was fairly easy since the first suspects were almost always servants or lodgers. A search of their personal goods was enough in some cases to secure the necessary evidence. If this failed to produce the required evidence then the next likely suspects were former servants or lodgers, especially if they had been seen loitering about in the vicinity. Dozens of former servants were caught in this way. Unlike total strangers to the house they knew where valuables were kept and the layout of the house.

Others were caught because they left incriminating evidence, most notably footprints. Burglars, sheep stealers and thieves were caught in this way, especially if it had been snowing. William Smith of Cydweli was apprehended in 1815 following a burglary in St. Ishmael, Gower, because the prosecutor traced 'the print of a man's shoes, having seven rows of nails uncommon in Wales'. Some criminals were just foolish. William Perkins of Swansea burgled a counting house barefooted in 1826 and stole some ham and a bottle of gin. Unfortunately for him he smashed a slate used in the counting house and trod on it in the dark causing his foot to bleed very badly. Bloodstains led to a nearby inn where he was found drunk with a bleeding foot. John

Humphreys of Meifod burgled the house of David Price, an old soldier, in 1815. Price had no idea who committed the crime until he saw Humphreys wearing his regimental uniform which 'had been cut off at one knee to accommodate his wooden leg.

The growth of newspapers meant that victims of crime could place adverts in the press describing when the goods had been stolen and giving a detailed description of the stolen goods. This was particularly successful in tracing stolen horses because they could not be disposed locally. Horse thieves who were caught as a direct result of newspaper adverts included Joseph Monkland in 1757 (he was transported for 14 years), Harry Richard Robert of Llangollen (sentenced to death on another indictment for horse stealing) and John Bliss in 1790 (transported for 7 years).

Handbills containing a description of a stolen horse and offering rewards for information leading to its recovery were posted up in towns were also successful sometimes. Sixteen year old Evan Pryce was especially unfortunate since he happened to be leading his stolen horse through Welshpool in 1819 when it was recognised by a person as he was actually pasting up the handbill. John Roberts was caught in exactly the same way in Nantmel, Radnorshire, in 1829. Both received the death sentence, but both were pardoned and instead Evan Pryce was sentenced to two years imprisonment and John Roberts to transportation to Australia for life.

A number of people put their faith in what were called cunning men or conjurors to discover who had stolen their goods. Cunning men, it was believed, had powers to cure people and animals as well as the ability to locate stolen items and to identify the thieves. From surviving evidence they were not very successful, but victims of crime still

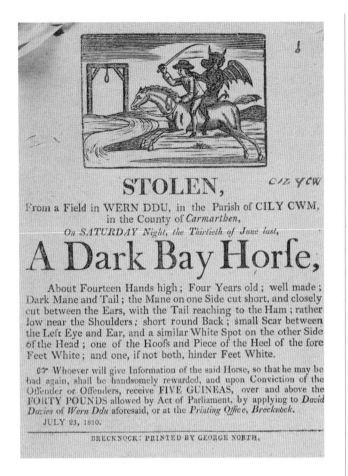

STOLEN,

From a Field in WERN DDU, *in the Parish of* CILY CWM, *in the County of Carmarthen,*

On SATURDAY *Night, the Thirtieth of June last,*

A Dark Bay Horse,

About Fourteen Hands high; Four Years old; well made; Dark Mane and Tail; the Mane on one Side cut short, and closely cut between the Ears, with the Tail reaching to the Ham; rather low near the Shoulders; short round Back; small Scar between the Left Eye and Ear, and a similar White Spot on the other Side of the Head; one of the Hoofs and Piece of the Heel of the fore Feet White; and one, if not both, hinder Feet White.

☞ Whoever will give Information of the said Horse, so that he may be had again, shall be handsomely rewarded, and upon Conviction of the Offender or Offenders, receive FIVE GUINEAS, over and above the FORTY POUNDS allowed by Act of Parliament, by applying to *David Davies* of *Wern Ddu* aforesaid, or at the *Printing Office, Brecknock.*

JULY 23, 1810.

BRECKNOCK: PRINTED BY GEORGE NORTH.

Handbill offering a reward for the recovery of a stolen horse, 23 July 1810. The handbill shows a horse thief being egged on by the devil straight to the gallows.
NLW, Court of Great Session Records 4/757/4/76.

turned to them for help. The fact that people believed in the cunning man's powers was sometimes enough for the culprit to give himself away. All of John Price's money was stolen from his house in 1788. He announced that he was going to consult a cunning man whereupon one of his servants immediately fled. Robert Darcy from Wrexham had a reputation as a cunning man. The following is a transcript of the evidence of a servant maid who consulted him on behalf of her master, Edward Phillips:

The examination of Catherine Taylor taken upon her oath the 30th day of Aprill 1740.

The examinant being sworn saith that Edward Phillips of Esclusham having lost a great parcel of linnen yarn (which was out in his orchard in order to be whitened and from thence upon Wednesday night the sixteenth of this month of April was feloniously taken by some person or persons unknown). Elizabeth Phillips, wife of the said Edward Phillips sent to this examinant and one Elizabeth Davies to goe to one Robert Darcy a cunning man and one that pretended to tell fortunes and help people to find out goods that were stolen. Accordingly this examinant then went with the said Elizabeth Davies to the said Robert Darcy, and asked him if he could give them any tideings of the said yarn that was stolen and who it was that stole it. He, the said Darcy, told them

that he was no conjurer but that he could tell by the planets who stole the yarn, and then produced a pack of cards and bid this examinant, `Cut them', which she did. And then he laid the cards in severall parcels upon the table, and then said it was a black man [that is, a man of dark complexion] that stooped in the shoulder and that used to trouble her, the said Elizabeth Phillips, for favours that stole the yarn, but that he would not tell them anymore without money, and bid them to send Edward Phillips or his wife there to him and he would tell them more. And this examinant hath heard that Edward Phillips did afterwards goe to consult the said Darcy about the said stolen yarn and gave Darcy money for his advice and further saith not.

Edward Phillips was very dissatisfied with Darcy's detective work. He sued him for obtaining money by false pretences. Darcy was convicted and fined.

Despite such a lack of success people continued to consult the cunning man well into the nineteenth century. Friends of Thomas Jones of Llansanffraid Glan Conwy discussed the possibility in 1824 of consulting a man called John Edwards to discover who had murdered Thomas's father. John Edwards, they agreed, 'had a reputation of being a conjurer and could show the guilty person in a glass.' Even after a professional police force had been established some people still preferred to consult a cunning man.

Sir Robert Peel established the Metropolitan Police Force in London in 1828. Wales already had numerous part time borough police forces in such towns as Merthyr and Haverfordwest, but the were few in numbers. Tenby had two policemen in 1836, Carmarthen five and Swansea seven. The Rural Police Act of 1839 enabled counties to establish their own professional police forces. Wales was quick to take advantage of the Act even though there was some opposition on grounds of cost and fear of policemen becoming spies as had happened - or so it was believed - in France. Five Welsh counties had created their own police forces by 1843. The 1839 Act did not compel counties to establish police forces but the County and Borough Police Act of 1856 did. The Act required all counties and large towns to set up professional police forces, with stations and cells to keep offenders. Many of the new chief constables were former military men and the influence of the military is obvious from the new police uniforms.

The effectiveness of the new police force was hotly debated at the time. It appears that the first generation police forces' task, as they saw it, was to reclaim the streets; clamping down on drunken behaviour, fights and troublesome beggars, and suppression of disturbances during fairs and elections. In the countryside police officers kept watch on where property was likely to be stolen such as hedgerows and railway lines. They also took into custody people in possession of poultry, watches and other goods that may have been stolen. They apprehended those who looked suspicious and were involved in almost a constant war against poachers.

NO POLICE!!

WELL DONE ABERYSTWYTH BOYS!

Your Month's Trial is past; and right nobly have you acquitted yourselves! Your behaviour has been admirable; your conduct deserves the utmost praise. The quiet, peaceable, and orderly state of the Town, is the greatest credit to you. It has been emphatically the MOST peaceable and happy Month enjoyed by the Town of Aberystwyth for Years! Even the Trees on the North Parade, so lately the objects of silly revenge, have not been touched. This is as it ought to be. Whoever destroys or injures them, is an Enemy to the Town, and an Abettor of the detested Police System! The fact of a Row of beautiful Trees growing there, cannot injure or annoy one single individual; nor could their removal benefit any one. There let them remain. Does not your voice already echo, Yes, there they shall remain!

Your conduct hitherto is a guarantee for the future; for to no one single act of disorder can even the finger of envy point! This has raised your character immeasurably; and proved, beyond the possibility of contradiction, that the Inhabitants of Aberystwyth do not require the surveillance of a couple of Bludgeon-men to keep them from becoming Pickpockets and Thieves. The question at the beginning of the Month was,

Police or No Police?

That problem has been solved; the question is answered. The Watch Committee appealed to the Town. The Inhabitants have responded—they have supplied the answer; and that answer is,

NO POLICE!!

The state of the Town for the last Month has proved to the satisfaction of the most timid and incredulous, that they were not required. As far as Aberystwyth is concerned, the Cutlasses and Truncheons of hired Spies may henceforth be consigned to oblivion in the Commissioners' Yard, along with rusty old Iron, rotten Timber, and broken Pipes, as perfectly useless Lumber, and Relics of bygone days.

PERSEVERE IN YOUR PRAISEWORTHY CONDUCT!

THE

£200

WILL BE SAVED,

And the Victory won!

April 6th, 1850.

E. WILLIAMS & SON, PRINTERS, ABERYSTWYTH.

Opposition to the new police force at Aberystwyth, 1850.
NLW POS27/7 PY 0831.

A Carmarthenshire police sergeant, [early 20 cent.].
NLW PZ 5186/12 (DCH113).

About 11 P.M. Saw a gang of Men by Cwrt Bridge, with blackened faces, and hoods over their heads. Armed with long Spears, and other bludgeons. "I advised them to go home, as they ware out for an unlawfull purpose". And was ordered if not turn back, would be killed on the Spot. One advanced in front, and held a Spear to my breast, in a threatening Manner, and making a strange noise in his throat. Then the others by headed by one, with word of "Fix Bayonets, Charge, Quick March." All ran up the hill on Llanfihangel road, when a distance up the hill they shouted home with the Devil. And I was pelted with Stones all the way home.

A policeman's lot. Dealing with a gang of poachers in Merioneth, 1878.
The Journal of P.C. John Hughes, Abergynolwyn.
Merioneth Record Office Z4/2/1.
By permission of Merioneth Record Office.

Friday March 30th 1877

about 10.20 pm I was on duty in John Town Hall I saw two men fighting between the Friends Arms public House and the Spite one of them had his Shirt off and the other had his Shirt on So soon as the one with his Shirt off saw me he ran up towards the Asylum I went after him but I could not catch him I returned back to Thomas Harris militia man age 28 he was drunk and his face all Blood I asked him to go home but he would not I then caught hold of him & took him into custody after I passed the park he became very violent he kicked and struck me several times I then was obliged to take out my Staff to him I struck him once on the leg afterwards with the assistance of Roberts Water Bailiff Handcuffed him he was very violent half way up to Picton's monument on the top of Picton's monument I met Sergeant Williams & he told Roberts Water Bailiff that he could go back he was using very abusive language all the way to the Station House he tore my top out I Helmet Broke the chain of my Whistle & lost my armlet the Scuffle property one Shilling and four Pence

J. C. John Arthur Hoy

Monday 16th April 1877

About 8 oClock this evening I was on duty in Red Street opposite Mr Joshua's Shop when I saw two Horses Galloping at full speed down Guild =hall square going in the direction of Lammas Street, there was no one on either of their backs one was an Entire Horse & the other a small pony. I went up Lammas Street at once and saw a large Crowd had Collected in front of the Plough Inn I ascertained that the Horses were Stopped by the Fusiliers Monument, and there was a Dispute amongst some Men, about taking charge of the Horse with great difficulty and with the Assistance of Inspector Henry I got the Horse from the Mob, and Delivered him to the Ostler of the Plough Inn About half an hour Afterwards I Saw a Man at the Plough, there was blood over his face he appeared to be under the influence of Liquor I assisted to remove him from the Bar to the Parlour, as the Crowd was pressing in the Bar, he told me that the Horse had Drawn him from off the Pony & that he was hurted a good deal

PC Evans No 3 States that About 7 pm he was on duty in Priory Street he saw a Man riding a Pony & leading an Entire Horse Back & fore Priory Street several times, he was under the Influence of Drink, and Cautioned him to take care of himself or else the Stallion would pull him down from off the Pony - he made no reply. He did not see him again, But can Identify him, he saw the Stallion & Pony coming down Priory Street, at full Galop in about half an Hour Afterwards with no one on the back, I have ascertained that the name of the Man who was in charge of the Stallion is Enoch Morgan Cappel Llanddewi nr Tregaron Cardiganshire

Reported by Ed Williams 188

A policeman's lot. Dealing with a runaway stallion, 1877.

Carmarthen Borough Police Report Book, 1876-1878.
By permission of Carmarthenshire Archives Service.

MISCONDUCT.

DATE.	OFFENCE.	BY WHOM REPORTED.	HOW DISPOSED OF.
13 Dec 1854	Not discovering that a man had been running about naked.		Fined 20/-
14 Oct. 1857	Not following the Instructions received from his Superint as to the pair of stays found on a Woman that was Murdered.		Fined 10/-
5 Oct 1858	Not being neat in his person and not having on his complete Police Dress.		Fined 20/-
15 June 1859	Not making proper inquiries as to the Trees destroyed at Marchogloryn		Fined 20/-
24 July 1868	Allowing a dog to come into the Court of Assizes -		Fined 5/-
6 Sept 1876	Not reporting to his Sup! that a man had been found dead in a wood at Pothyrhyd.		Fined 20/-
			Superannuate

Career record of a member of the Carmarthenshire constabulary.
Carmarthenshire Police Record and Defaulters Book.
By permission of Carmarthenshire Archives Service.

'Mug shots' of prisoners at Aberystwyth before and after the use of fingerprinting.
NLW MS 23203B, ff. 2,22v.

Description and previous convictions of
Arthur Davies Alias George Williams etc
born at Abertillery in 1887. Trade, Collier. Height 5 ft 5½ inches
Complexion Fresh. Hair, Brown. Eyes Brown.

Sentence	Court and Place State if at Ass, Sess, or Polic		Date			Offence of which prisoner was actually found guilty	Full Christian and Surnames
1 day & 6 Strokes	P.S. Blaina	8	1	97	Stg money from till	George Williams
Fined 20/9 costs	P.S. Abertillery	22	6	04	Stg a fowl	" "
1 Month	P.S. Tredegar	28	11	05	Stg a watch & chain	" "
3 Months	P.S. Mountain Ash	17	1	06	Stg a pair of boots	" "
2 Months H.L.	P.S. Abertillery	20	6	06	Stg a pair of boots	" "
2 Months H.L. Consec	" "	"	"	"	Stg a bible	" "
3 Months H.L.	" "	7	11	06	Lodging out	" "
2 " H.L.	P.S. Pontypool	20	4	07	Stg a suit of clothes	" "
2 " H.L. Consec	" "	"	"	"	Stg a bicycle	" "
2 " H.L.	" "	"	"	"	Stg a bicycle	" "
6 weeks H.L.	P.S. Swansea	13	11	07	Stg 4 Mufflers	" "
9 Months H.L.	P.S. Builth	24	2	08	Stg watch & Chain Brooch	William Davies
1.6 Month H.L.	P.C. Hereford City	19	10	09	Drunk & Disorderly	Arthur Davies
1 " " Consec	" " "	"	"	"	Assault Police	" "
6 " " H.L.	P.S. Abertillery	20	12	09	" "	Geo Williams
3 " " H.L. Consec	" "	"	"	"	" "	" "
6 " " H.L.	" Monmouth	21	9	10	Stg Silve chain	" "
6 " " H.L. Consec	" "	"	"	"	Assault Police	" "
	4 Summary convictions for sleeping out drunkenness &c						
3.6 Months H.L.	P.C. Hereford City	17	1	12	Stg a pair of boots	Arthur Davies, Al, George Williams
6 Months H.L.	P.S. Gloucester City	24	4	12	Stg pr boots knife & Apron	George Williams
14 days H.L.	P.C. Port Talbot	8	1	13	Sleeping out	" "
1 Month	P.C. Birkenhead	2	2	14	Begging	William James
7 days	P.C. Stratford on Avon	11	7	14	Obscene Language	Henry Jones
1 Month	P.S. Aberystwyth	13	5	16	Begging	George Williams
1 " Consec	" "	"	"	"	Assault Police	" "

Previous convictions of one Arthur Davies.
NLW MS 23203B, f.111.

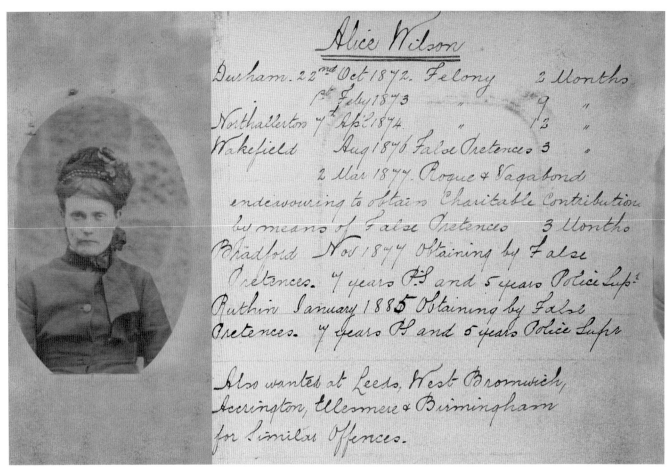

Police 'mug shot' of Alice Wilson and previous convictions circulated in the Police Gazette, [c. 1885].
Denbighshire Record Office QAD/AG 72-3.
By permission of Denbighshire Record Office.

The new police force was not without its problems. Turnover among the new officers was high because so many either resigned or were sacked because they either could not cope or broke the strict police discipline. Many were sacked for not reporting crimes, visiting brothels and especially for drinking while on duty.

It took time to create a disciplined police force and for the new force to be accepted. Eventually, even those who opposed their establishment in the first place changed their minds. The new police force was a preventative force not a detecting one, that had to wait until the CID (Criminal Investigation Department) was set up. However, some new developments did help them greatly such as fingerprinting, photography and the setting up of the *Police Gazette* which circulated names of habitual criminals released from prisons together with their descriptions and previous convictions.

BEFORE THE COURTS

Today, one of the fundamental principals of the criminal law is that a prisoner is innocent until proved guilty. Until the early part of the nineteenth century this was not the case: the court assumed that a prisoner was guilty and that if he was innocent he ought to be able to prove it by his evidence. He had to prove that the prosecutor was wrong. This was not easy since the prisoner did not have a lawyer to represent him, nor did the victim of the crime. Lawyers representing

both the prosecutor and the defendant were only gradually allowed into court roughly from the mid to late eighteenth century. As far back as the reign of Mary Tudor in the sixteenth century the courts assumed that a prisoner was guilty and not innocent. Justices of the peace were only required to take down evidence of witnesses most likely to prove the crime. Justices of the peace often highlighted the most damning evidence against an accused, as did some nineteenth century judges when they took notes during the trial.

At the start of the criminal trial each prisoner had to plead guilty or not guilty. A very small minority refused to plead at all (called 'standing mute') in order to prevent the Crown from taking their lands or possessions if they were convicted of felony or treason. The courts could not allow this and the prisoner was subjected to a terrible form of torture in order to force him to plead. He was taken to a dungeon, chained and spread-eagled to the floor and pressed with more and more iron weights until he either agreed to plead, or until he died. This barbaric practice, which could last for two or three days, was not outlawed until 1772.

Since there were no lawyers present in court, witnesses were examined and cross-examined by the judge. He knew beforehand who was to be tried and what the charges were because he had been given a list of all the prisoners to appear before him and for what offences. This list, called a

22

William Spiggott being pressed in Newgate, 1769. The person actually being pressed is someone else. Spiggott was never in Newgate and was never pressed because he pleaded not guilty.
NLW MS 23206D, p.74.

was a forensic cross-examination of sorts because Lilly was on horseback when he was shot and Owen was on foot. Owen claimed that the bullet had entered Lilly's body vertically, thus he could not possibly have fired the shot. The jury refused to believe him and he was executed on Pensarn hill outside Carmarthen in April 1747.

A prisoner could also say something on his own behalf after the witnesses had been examined. Again, very few said anything at all. Some, however, produced character witnesses on their behalf at the end of the trial, and there is no doubt that such witnesses were crucial in deciding the outcome of the trial. The prisoner wanted to prove that he was a hardworking, trusted and sober member of the community and not an idle layabout with no means to support himself and his family, and that the offence he had committed was totally out of character, possibly the result of overwhelming temptation to which most others would have succumbed. David Hughes of Holyhead was charged in 1830 with stealing a horse. He was acquitted because 'numerous and respectable witnesses...had given such favourable testimony to the character of the accused'. The jury believed his story - that he had purchased the horse at Caernarfon fair.

Most trials lasted little more than a quarter of an hour. William Dillwyn of Walthamstow was shocked by the speed of proceedings when he sat at the new Old Bailey to watch and listen to criminal trials.

After every prisoner had been tried, those found not guilty were released; those convicted were brought individually to court to hear the judge pronounce sentence upon them. When the death sentence was handed down the judge would wear his famous black cap and give a brief lecture to the prisoner about the grave nature of his offence and why society would be better off without him, before exhorting him to seek forgiveness from God. Such speeches could move the judge and the court spectators to tears. When Justice Park delivered the sentence of death on James Harry for murdering his wife in 1817, most of the 800 spectators were reduced to tears apart, that is, from James Harry himself. Monoglot Welsh speakers sometimes had the dubious distinction of being sentenced to death twice. According to a Herefordshire newspaper, some of those convicted of the murder of William Powell of Glanareth, Carmarthenshire, in 1770, had to be brought back to court so that the sentence could be translated into Welsh for them, because they were unaware that the Judge had actually sentenced them to death. Richard Rowlands had to be brought back to court in 1862 after the judge passed the sentence of death on him because he had not understood the sentence. When it was translated, he collapsed in a heap and wept uncontrollably.

However, before the death sentence was passed prisoners could still avoid the hangman's noose even at this late stage. Until 1706, if a prisoner could recite a verse from the Bible, usually the first verse of Psalm 51 (popularly called the neck verse) he could be granted what was called benefit of clergy and avoid being executed provided this was his first offence.

calendar of prisoners, was handed over to the judge together with the written evidence of witnesses taken when an offence took place or when the prisoner was arrested before the court sat.

Prisoners had the right to examine witnesses themselves. Few did so. They were often illiterate, often ill from being imprisoned for months in unhealthy gaols, and they did not know what evidence witnesses would produce until the moment it was given in court. They had no chance then to prepare their own defence. There were a few exceptions to this pattern of passive prisoners, and one of the most remarkable was William Owen, a notorious smuggler from Cardigan, who was charged in 1747 with the murder of one James Lilly by shooting him with a pistol. He cross-examined every witness produced in court who saw James Lilly's body and asked them all whether the fatal bullet had entered Lilly's belly vertically or at an upward angle. This

GLAMORGANSHIRE.

A CALENDAR

OF THE

Criminal Prisoners,

Confined in His Majesty's Gaol, at Cardiff:

Who are to be Tried or Disposed of, at the Great Sessions to be held at Cardiff. for the said County;

On SATURDAY, the 23rd of AUGUST, 1828.

BEFORE THE

Honorable N. G. CLARKE, Esquire,

AND THE

Honorable ROBERT MATHEW CASBERD, Esquire.

R. F. JENNER, Esquire, Sheriff.

No.	Name.	Age.	Trade, &c.	OFFENCE.	Sentence.
1.	Benjamin Harris,	28,	Labourer,	Committed 19th June, 1828, by J. B. Bruce, Esq. charged on the oaths of Evan Williams and others, with breaking into his house, situate at Newbridge, and stealing a Coat and other wearing apparel therefrom.	*Guilty Sentence , Death Recorded*
2.	Thomas Morgan,	20,	Boatman,	Committed 26th July, 1828, by The Rev. G. Thomas, Clerk, charged upon the oaths of William Rees and others, with having stolen three Iron Chains, of the value of ten shillings, the goods and chattels of The Marquis of Bute.	*Guilty one year imprisonment*
3.	Evan Smith,	32,	Miller,	Committed 2nd August, 1828, by F. Fredricks, Esq. and The Rev. T. Gronow, Clerk, charged on the oath of John Thomas, with having received several sums of Money to the amount of fourteen shillings, for and on his account, and did fraudulently and feloniously embezzle and secrete the same.	*acquitted*
4.	John Davies,	23,	Smith,	Committed 9th August, 1828, by W. Forman, Esq. charged on the oaths of Giles Williams and others, with having feloniously stolen one silver Watch, from the dwelling house of the said Giles Williams, situate at Hyrwain, in the parish of Aberdare, his property.	*Pleaded Guilty —*

Calendar of prisoners awaiting trial at Glamorgan, 1828, with notes of verdicts and sentences added by a clerk of the court.
NLW, Court of Great Sessions Records 4/639/4/37.

many people about him, and he was alive: He declared much to the same purpose as the other Witness. ___

Judge. Prisoner have you any Questions to ask this Witness. ___

Prisoner. Yes, my Lords with Submission I have Several Questions to ask him ___ If your Lordships please to ask him, if I Seemed to have any anger at Lilly when in his House. ___

Witness. No not the least, that I could See or hear, but Seemed very

very loving with another ___

Prisoner. How was the wound in his head, do you think he had that Wound on him in your House. ___

Witness. No, he had not.

Prisoner. How was the Wound in the Breast, and was his Coat and waistcoat Burnt ___

Witness. His Coat and waistcoat was Burnt, and the Wound was directly in. ___

Judge. Gentlemen for the Crown have you any more Witness to call.

Counsel

William Owen's cross-examination of a witness during his trial for murder, 1747.
NLW MS 21834B, ff.138-9.

The Sentence of the Law is, and this Court doth order and adjudge, that you Sarah Davies be taken from hence to the prison from whence you came, & that you be drawn thence upon a hurdle ~~through~~ to the place of Execution on the fifth day of September Instant, & that you be there hanged by the neck until you are dead & that your body, when dead, be taken down, & be dissected & anatomized. And may God have mercy upon your Soul. ___

Justice Heywood was in the habit of drafting sentences of death before trials had been concluded. This is his draft for Sarah Davies, 1811.
Fortunately for her, she was acquitted.
NLW MS 204D.

Mr. Juſtice Hardinge's Addreſs to the Convicts, who were tried before him at the Cardiff Great Seſſion, *upon the 8th. of April* 1801.

SAMUEL HILL,
JAMES LUKE,
AARON WILLIAMS,

           Painful as it muſt ever be for a Judge to paſs the ſentence of death upon thoſe who have legally forfeited their lives, I never have experienced in this duty ſuch peculiar feelings of perſonal oppreſſion, as in contemplating *your* fate.

  Upon other occaſions the malice of the Culprit's heart, or the diſhoneſty of his life, (as well as of the particular act which is capitally charged) braces the mind and the nerves to the duty of conſigning, by judicial ſentence, the offender to his doom.

  But three individuals are now before me, who 'till the moment of this dreadful outrage, appear to have led at leaſt very unimpeached, and perhaps virtuous lives.

  A ſudden famine, or ſcarcity of grain, which of courſe made proviſions dear, to an extreme, gave the firſt alarm to your feelings ; and many (I have no doubt) enliſted under the banner of artful incendiaries, with a fatally miſcalculated hope, that by *terror alone*, without *actual miſchief*, a reform of the market price would be accompliſhed by their ſpirit.

  The cowardice of the inhabitants, and the indolence, or blind credulity, of the Magiſtrates, after the firſt notice of a concerted enterprize againſt the peace of the Town, a want of ſpirit in ſome of the parties injured, and the general defect of police (in a part of the world that requires it the moſt) encouraged you to perſevere.

  Heated by your paſſions, and by liquor, you were more and more inflamed, at every new ſtep, againſt the peaceful neighbours, 'till the whole Town was at the mercy of undiſciplined violence.

  It is true that no acts of *perſonal cruelty* appear to have taken place.

  But alas ! at a moment like this, and with a reference to ſome very important features of your conduct, in a political view, I am deeply concerned at the intelligence which I muſt impart, that I ſee no ground of hope for your exemption from capital puniſhment; tho' I ſhall rather give my *opinion* to the King, who is the fountain of mercy, than determine your fate myſelf.

  I lament (and ſo muſt every obſerver who looks at the *moral* differences of guilt) that many of your incendiaries, and ringleaders, are to eſcape from *your* puniſhment.

  Yet the warning of this very difference is not without its uſe. It will teach the careleſs minds and ſpirits of men, what a peril they incur, in liſtening to thoſe who make them act as the inſtruments, and ſervile miniſters, of unlawful aſſemblies, for any purpoſe whatever.

  The circumſtances which imperiouſly demand an example of ſignal juſtice, and which have devoted *you* as its victims, are theſe.

  We have the heavieſt of all calamities impending over this land ; an expenſive, and ruinous, though neceſſary, war ;—taxes that weigh down the people, and ſuch a dearth of proviſion for the neceſſaries of life, as this iſland has never experienced.

  At ſuch a moment, it is the duty of the legiſlature to do what they are doing to relieve the poor, as much, and as well, as human wiſdom can alleviate their diſtreſs.

  But it is no leſs the duty of Juries, of Judges, and of the Executive Power, to guard the lives, and properties of men, againſt that *worſt of all tyrants,*—a *rabble unlawfully aſſembled.*

  It was repreſented by the Counſel for your proſecutors, that you, and others of your party, made uſe of the general calamity, as a mere colour, and pretence for general havock, and pillage.

  I do not approve the diſtinction : for whether it was the *colourable*, or the *real* ground of your conduct, makes not a feather of difference in the guilt ; and it would be dangerous to intimate, that where a hope to reduce the market price is the *ſole* object, a rioter will be deemed innocent, who purſues that object by force.

Address of Justice Harding when sentencing three rioters to death, 1801.
NLW, Bute Papers L48/57.

To the Sheriff of the County of Monmouth, his Undersheriff, and to the Keeper of his Majesty's Gaol of the said County.

Let the Execution of John James and William Jenkins who were convicted before me at the last Assizes for the County of Monmouth, of Burglary, be stayed until his Majesty's pleasure be further known herein, and for so doing, this shall be your sufficient Authority. Given under my hand at Gloucester this tenth day of April 1835. —

J W Park.

Stay of execution of John James and William Jenkins convicted of burglary, 1835.
NLW, Sir Leonard Twiston Davies Papers 6918.

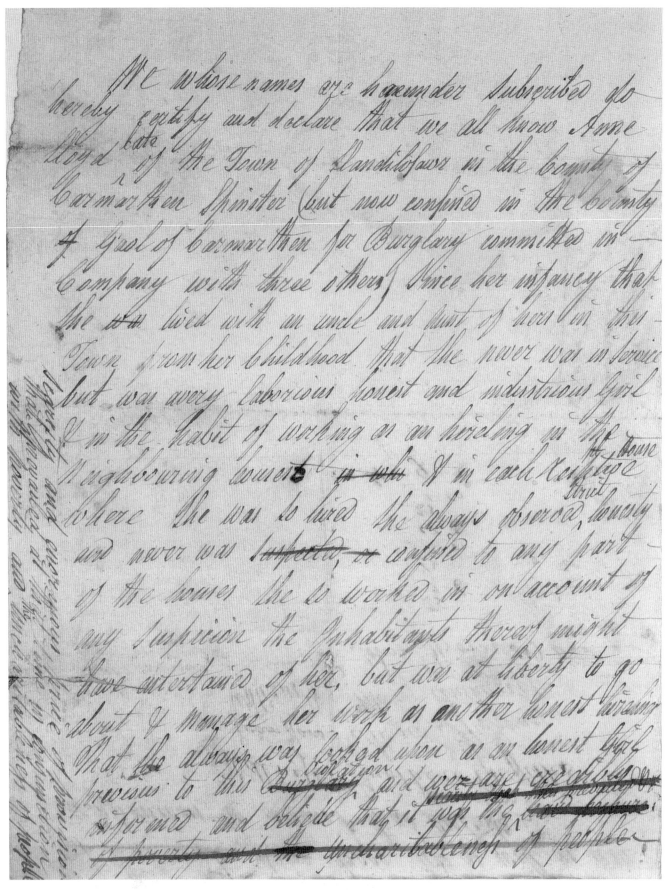

We whose names are hereunder subscribed do
hereby certify and declare that we all know Anne
Lloyd late of the Town of Llandilofawr in the County of
Carmarthen Spinster (but now confined in the County
Gaol of Carmarthen for Burglary committed in
Company with three others) Since her infancy that
she was lived with an uncle and aunt of hers in this
Town from her Childhood that she never was in service
but was a very laborious honest and industrious Girl
& in the habit of working as an hireling in the
neighbouring houses & in each House
where she was to lived she always observed honesty
and never was suspected, or confined to any part
of the houses she to worked in on account of
any suspicion the Inhabitants thereof might
have entertained of her, but was at liberty to go
about & manage her work as another honest servant
That she always was looked upon as an honest Girl
previous to this Burglary, and we are firmly
informed and believe that it was the
of poverty

Draft certificate testifying to the good character of Anne Lloyd awaiting trial with three others for burglary, [1801].
NLW MS 21411E, f. 69.

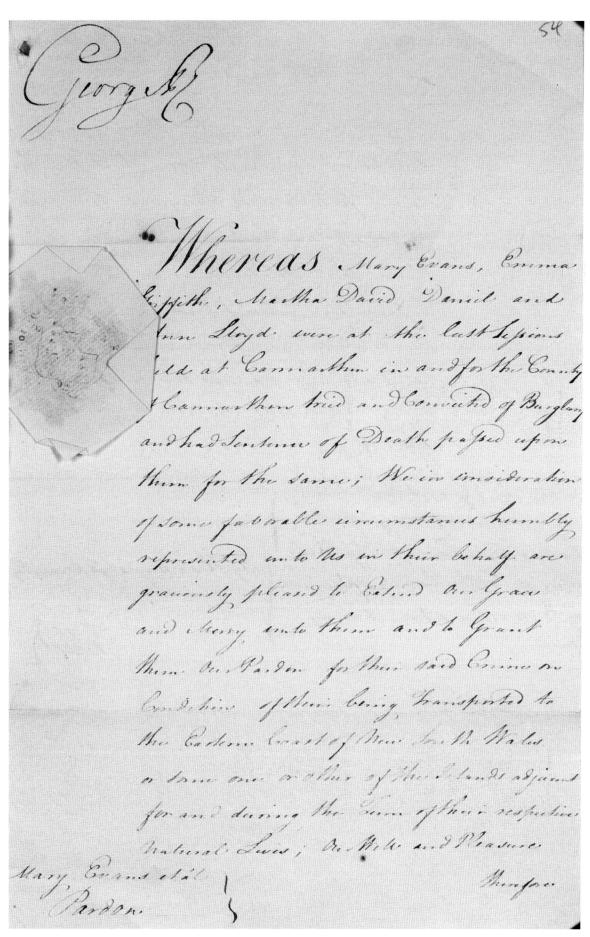

George R

Whereas Mary Evans, Emma Griffith, Martha David, Daniel and Ann Lloyd were at the last Sessions held at Carmarthen in and for the County of Carmarthen tried and Convicted of Burglary and had Sentence of Death passed upon them for the same; We in consideration of some favorable circumstances humbly represented unto Us in their behalf are graciously pleased to Extend Our Grace and Mercy unto them and to Grant them Our Pardon for their said Crime on Condition of their being Transported to the Eastern Coast of New South Wales or some one or other of the Islands adjacent for and during the term of their respective natural Lives; Our Will and Pleasure therefore

Mary Evans et al.
Pardon.

Pardon to Anne Lloyd and her accomplices for burglary, 1801.
NLW, Court of Great Sessions Records 4/753/2/54.

29

Instead of being hanged he would be branded on his thumb. This escape route was not available to all offenders, however; no one could claim benefit of clergy for particular offences such as murder, burglary, shoplifting and some other serious felonies. Most poor prisoners could not read, and it is apparent that other literate prisoners taught them to learn the neck verse off by heart. If a judge felt that a prisoner should not be granted benefit clergy, he would sometimes ask the prisoner to recite another verse. Most, one suspects, could not. From 1706, this literacy test was abolished but benefit of clergy remained available for the first offence.

Even after the death sentence had been pronounced, convicted prisoners unable to claim benefit of clergy could still avoid being hanged if the judge recommended him to the King for a pardon. In such cases the judge would issue a formal order to the sheriff to postpone or stay execution until the King's decision had been received. Judges usually recommended pardons to those of previously good character; to the very young and very old prisoners; and to those whom they thought had been wrongly convicted by the jury. Other factors that influenced their decision were a petition from local people, particularly people of influence, to pardon the prisoner usually because he or she was a trustworthy person from a good and respectable family. However, very few prisoners granted pardons walked out of gaol free men or women. Almost all pardons substituted the death sentence with that of imprisonment or transportation or, if Britain was at war, to join the army or navy.

PUNISHMENT

Minor criminals were sentenced to be whipped or sent to the pillory for an hour. Until the late eighteenth century whipping was carried out in public to shame the offender and his family and to deter others. The offender was tied to

mud, sticks and stones. Some were very badly wounded and a very small number were actually killed. In the end this was the reason why the pillory was abolished in 1837. People were being handed out punishments that the courts had not authorised.

Before 1718 when the Transportation Act was passed by Parliament, judges could only sentence criminal offenders to be executed, branded if they were allowed benefit of clergy, or whipping. Transportation to colonial America or later to Australia appealed to the authorities because it was a simple, but very permanent solution, to the problem of ridding society of dangerous and undesirable persons. Transportation rapidly became the alternative to the death penalty from 1718. It was to last until 1868.

It has been estimated that 56,000 convicts were exiled to the American colonies between 1718 and 1785, or a quarter of all emigrants from Britain to America during these years. When transportation to America was no longer possible after the American War of Independence, convicts were sent to Australia from 1787. A staggering 160,000 were sent there from Britain between 1787 and 1868, of which 2,200 came from Wales. Few ever returned. John Frost, leader of the Chartist uprising in Newport in 1839, and David Davies, (Dai'r Cantwr) one of the Rebecca rioters, were rare exceptions.

The trip to America took between six and eight weeks during which time the convicts were held in horrific conditions. They were chained below deck in cages, and suffered from lack of food, clothing and fresh air. Some convicts given insufficient rations of water became so thirsty that they drank their own urine. Deaths were frequent. The journey to Australia was even more gruelling. It has been estimated that a fifth of all convicts died during the long journey to Australia. This is the account of Thomas

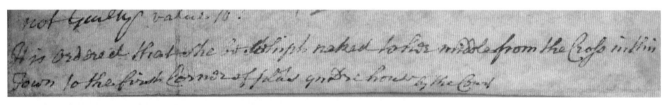

Order of the Merioneth Quarter Sessions to whip Margaret Richard, convicted of stealing an old pair of shoes and a handkerchief, 1763.
Merioneth Record Office ZQS/H/1763/12.
By permission of Merioneth Record Office.

a cart and whipped from part of a town to another part. The amount of punishment could depend then on how fast or how slow the horse was going and the mood of the person handing out the punishment.

An offender sentenced to do penance in a pillory was exhibited on a platform with his hands and head fixed to a wooden structure, with details of his offence written on a piece of paper placed on his head. The point of this type of punishment was not only to deter the offender and others buy also to make his identity known. It was a warning to the public not to trust this man. Many were pilloried for fraud and cheating, others for sexual offences. The reaction of the crowd could be brutal. Offenders were often pelted with

Milburn (quoted by Robert Hughes in his book *The Fatal Shore*) of his journey to Australia with the Second Fleet in 1790:

'[We were] chained two and two together and confined to the hold during the whole course of the long voyage...[We] were scarcely allowed a sufficient quantity of victuals to keep us alive, and scarcely any water...When any of our comrades that were chained to us died, we kept it a secret as long as we could for the smell of a dead body, in order to get their allowance of provision, and many a time I have been glad to eat the poultice that was put to my leg for perfect hunger. I was chained to Humphrey Davies who died when we were

Order of the court empowering justices of the peace to contract for the transportation of John Jones convicted of fraud, 1790.
NLW, Court of Great Sessions Records 14/14, f. 161.

half way, and I lay beside his corpse about a week and got his allowance'.

Most Welsh convicts were transported to the American colonies or to Australia from London. Arrangements had to be made for their removal from Welsh gaols to London. This was usually done by the courts appointing named justices of the peace to contract for their removal.

Life as a convict was hard and brutal; beatings and punishments were commonplace. It seems, however, that the pain of separation from family, friends and neighbours was even worse than physical punishment. We can experience this despair felt by convicts from ballads written by them.

David Davies wrote three ballads: the first when he was in Carmarthen gaol awaiting transportation, the other two from his exile in Australia. Readers are asked to consider (and learn from) his desperate situation. He longs for his beloved area where he was born and bred in Glamorgan and

Monmouthshire, for his family and friends and for Wales. His longing only gets worse during his exile where he is condemned to work in stenching sulphur mines. He abandoned God and he has been forced to abandon everything that he loves with no hope of ever returning. Much to his delight no doubt, he was pardoned in 1854 three years after he wrote his last ballad. He duly returned to Wales but not to a very happy ending. He lived the life of a tramp and died twenty years later when he was burned to death when the barn he was sleeping in caught fire from his pipe after he had fallen asleep, drunk.

However, ballads such as these are not always what they appeared. The ballad of Lewis Rees who, along with his sister Anne, was sentenced at Dolgellau Quarter Sessions in 1854 to seven years transportation for theft is a good example. The ballad was not written by Lewis himself but by the poet who based it on a letter sent to him by Rees as he was being moved to London to await transportation. The ballad conveys his feeling of pain, despair and personal tragedy at being forced to leave his relations, friends,

CAN HIRAETHLON

DAVID DAVIES,

DAI'R CANTWR,

Pan yn Garcharor yn amser Rebecca.

Ton—Roslyn Castle.

Drych i fyd wyf i fod,
Collais glod all'twn gael,
Tost yw'r nòd, dyrnod wael,
I'w gafael ddaeth a mi.
Yn fy is'nctyd dryglyd ddaeth,
Yn lle rhyddid caethfyd maith,
'Chwanegwyd er fy ngofid,
Alltud wyf, ar ddechreu'm taith.
Ca'm danfon o fy ngwlad,
Ty fy'nhad, er codiad tirion,
I blith y duon gôr
Dros y môr o'm goror gron.
O ! 'r fath ddychryn imi ddaeth !
Alltud hir—gyr hyn fu'n gaeth
Dros ugain o flynyddoedd—
Tost yw'r modd—cystudd maith!

2. Can' ffarwel i fy ngwlad
Anwyl fad, fu wrth fy modd;
Aml les g'es ar g'odd
Rhwng dy wych aberoedd di;
O ffarwel i Walia gron,
Ei dolydd glwys a'i llwyni llon,
Heb bryder gwn mai Prydain
Yw gardd y byd i gyd o'r bron.
Hil Gomer mwy ffarwel,
I dir Babel fe'm danfonir;
Dros hely mae fy nhaith
Arw faith, Duw fo i mi'n fur.

David Davies's ballad written in Carmarthen gaol awaiting transportation to Australia, [1843x1844].

32

CAN NEWYDD

SEF CWYN

LEWIS REES,

A'I

Chwaer Ann,

Cyn cychwyn eu Halltudiaeth i
phordd o Lundain, rhai a Alltud-
iwyd o herwydd eu lladrad o
Ddolgellau, Gorphenaf 25, 1854.

Cenir ar *"Belisle March."*

Yn awr gyfeillion o un galon,
Yn gyson nos a dydd,
De'wch i wrando arnai'n cwyno
Heb flino yn ddi-gudd;
Clywch fy mhrofiad mewn caethiwed,
Yr y'm mewn galar dwys,
Yn hiraethu a galaru
Am Gymru landeg lwys,
Am Gymru mae fy mryd,
A'i harddwch oll i gyd,
O na ddeuwn eto iddi
O'm holl drueni drud,
Yr y'm ni yma'n anniddanol,
Yn gwneud annynol nad;
Eto'n methu codi i fynu,
I ganfod fy hen wlad,
Mae'n galed arnom ni
Rwy'n dyweud y gwir i chwi,
Digalon hynod bob diwrnod,
Yw i fy chwaer a fi,
Heb un gobaith gwaredigaeth
Dd'od o'r galedwaith hwn,
Hyd nes talu'r ffyrling eitha'
A'r olaf oll mi wn.

Ballad of Lewis Rees based on a letter written by him on his way to London to be transported to Australia, 1854. The ballad is a fake.

neighbours, Merioneth and Wales forever. It is a piece of pure fabrication since - as the calendar of Merioneth prisoners clearly shows - Lewis Rees could not write a single word.

By the time Dai'r Cantwr left Australia conditions had greatly improved. Indeed, it was rumoured in Britain that people were now deliberately committing offences so that they could be sent to Australia. Schemes were also afoot to send wives and children of convicts there provided the convicts had been well behaved. Criticism of transportation had been growing for years and finally Australians themselves put an end to it. This meant that prison sentences became the chief means of punishing wrongdoers.

Eighteenth century prisons were never designed to hold long-term prisoners. Their function was to hold prisoners until the assizes met. The prisons themselves were often appalling places, run by individuals for a profit, usually by selling food and alcohol to the prisoners. Prisons were unhealthy and damp, with no toilets, running water or sewage system. Death from what was called gaol fever was common. Houses of Correction which were first established during the reign of Queen Elizabeth were no better. They had been established, however, to reform those described as the able bodied poor who refused to work such as vagrants, the idle, and the disorderly by punishment and discipline. This concept of reforming people was not the purpose of prisons that were designed merely to hold prisoners until their trial.

In both prisons and houses of correction discipline was lax, gaolers were frequently negligent and the gaols were simply not secure enough. Not surprisingly escapes were common. Items used to saw chains or to climb over walls were smuggled into prisons without too much difficulty. William Hudson escaped from Beaumaris gaol in 1774 with the help of two knives smuggled into the prison 'hacked and cut into the forms of saws to enable the prisoner to cut irons'. Margaret Jones escaped unrecognised from Haverfordwest gaol by wearing clothes that her children had smuggled in to her.

The most famous Welsh escapee was John Jones (Coch Bach Y Bala), known in England as 'The Little Welsh Terror' or 'The Little Turpin.' He spent most of his adult life behind bars, but he became famous for his prison escapes. He escaped from Ruthin gaol in 1879 by somehow managing to open his cell door and three other doors before walking out through the main gate. He escaped from Bala but failed to break out of Caernarfon gaol in 1900 whilst all the prison staff were celebrating the relief of Mafeking. He was more successful in 1913 when he managed to escape from Ruthin gaol for a second time by digging a hole in his cell. With a rope made from bedclothes he lowered himself so that he was able to climb on to the roof of the prison chapel and kitchen before climbing over the prison wall. The escape ended in tragedy. Five days later, Wil, half starved and wearing only prison underpants, a sack and a greatcoat, was seen by a 19 year old student named Reginald Jones Bateman of Eyarth Hall who was out shooting partridges. Bateman, who recognised Wil, tried to persuade him to give himself up. Wil refused. Bateman then thought Wil was pulling a gun from under his coat and he

shot him in the leg. Wil died less than five minutes after the shot was fired.

The terrible conditions in prisons and the efforts of penal reformers like John Howard eventually led to the reform of British prisons. Howard visited every gaol in England and Wales and his report was very damning. He recommended more space, better food, paid gaolers, and the separation of male from female prisoners, and separation of debtors from prisoners. During the next fifty years new prisons were built with a uniform system of how prisoners were to be kept in custody. Convicts had to wear a uniform with badges (as marks of humiliation), were to be fed inferior food, and were to be kept in solitary confinement. They were to be punished for breaking prison rules and they were to be kept at work almost every day of the year except Sunday and this labour was to be of the hardest and most repetitive kind such as treading the wheel and picking oakum (separating out old fibres from tarred ropes so that they could be re-used).

While prison conditions were healthier the prison regime was much stricter. This was made even tougher by the adoption of new methods of prison discipline imported from the United States called the Silent System and the Separate System. Both were designed to ensure that prisoners did not communicate with each other by word, gesture or sign. Both systems - though never adopted in all British prisons - were also intended to break down a prisoner's spirit. Confined in solitary all day, it was believed that a prisoner with the help of his Bible and the urgings of the prison chaplain would realise the error of his ways and repent. What often happened, however, was that prisoners went mad, suffered a nervous breakdown, committed suicide, or assaulted the chaplain.

Some new prisons were built using Jeremy Bentham's plan called the Panopticon. Prisoners could also be watched all the time when they were outside their cells in this type of prison. It was adopted on a small scale in prisons such as Ruthin.

The ultimate punishment of course was death. Executions – held in public until 1868 - were mass spectator events. Crowds of between 35-40,000 were not uncommon at Tyburn, and it was estimated that 100,000 gathered to watch the beheading of the Cato Street conspirators for treason in 1820. In Wales the crowds were much smaller of course. Nevertheless, Welsh newspapers estimated that 10,000 turned out to watch the execution of David Evans at Carmarthen in 1829, between 20,000-25,000 for the execution of Thomas Thomas at Brecon in 1845, and 25,000 for the hanging of Robert Coe in Swansea in 1866. And they had plenty of opportunity to watch. In England, it has been estimated that 67 persons were executed annually between 1805 and 1814. Between 1730 and 1830, somewhere between 450 and 500 persons were hanged in Wales.

Execution crowds in London were far more boisterous than elsewhere. Welsh crowds said prayers with the officiating minister and then silence only broken by the shrieks of women when the prisoner was hanged, but they did make their views known. Murderers were reviled. Thomas Webborn who was hanged in 1799 for the murder of his eight year old servant

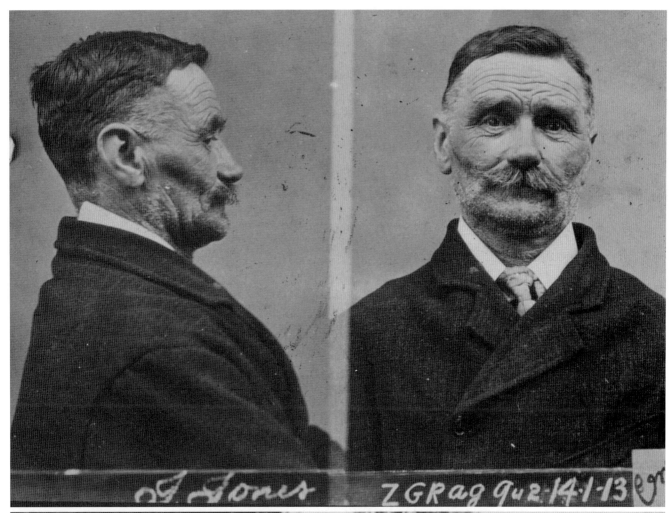

Police photograph of John Jones (Coch Bach Y Bala) and a photograph of his funeral, 1913.
Merioneth Record Office ZS/34M3-4.
By permission of Merioneth Record Office.

DIETARY

Recommended by the Secretary of State for Prisoners confined in the Merioneth County Gaol.

CLASS 1.

For Prisoners sentenced to any term not exceeding Seven Days with or without hard Labour :—

MALES.

BREAKFAST,—6 ounces of Bread.

DINNER,
- Monday, Wednesday, and Friday, } 6 ounces of Bread, and 6 ounces of Indian Meal Pudding.
- Tuesday, Thursday, and Saturday, } 6 ounces of Bread, and 8 ounces of Potatoes.
- Sunday, ... 8 ounces Bread.

SUPPER,—6 ounces of Bread.

FEMALES.

BREAKFAST,—5 ounces of Bread.

DINNER,
- Monday, Wednesday, and Friday, } 5 ounces of Bread, and 4 ounces of Indian Meal Pudding.
- Tuesday, Thursday, and Saturday, } 5 ounces of Bread, and 6 ounces of Potatoes.
- Sunday, ... 6 ounces of Bread.

SUPPER,—5 ounces of Bread.

CLASS 2.

For Prisoners who have been in the Gaol more than Seven Days, and not more than One Month, after Conviction :—

MALES

BREAKFAST,—6 ounces of Bread, and 1 pint of Oatmeal Gruel.

DINNER,
- Monday, Wednesday, and Friday, } 6 ounces of Bread, and 8 ounces of Indian Meal Pudding.
- Tuesday, Thursday, and Saturday, } 6 ounces of Bread, and 12 ounces of Potatoes.
- Sunday, ... 8 ounces of Bread, and 1 ounce of Cheese.

SUPPER,—6 ounces of Bread.

FEMALES

BREAKFAST,—5 ounces of Bread, and 1 pint of Oatmeal Gruel.

DINNER,
- Monday, Wednesday, and Friday, } 5 ounces of Bread, and 6 ounces of Indian Meal Pudding.
- Tuesday, Thursday, and Saturday, } 5 ounces of Bread, and 8 ounces of Potatoes.
- Sunday, ... 6 ounces of Bread, and 1 ounce of Cheese.

SUPPER,—5 ounces of Bread.

NOTE.—*When Prisoners of this Class are employed at hard Labour, they will have 1 ounce of Cheese extra on Sundays, and a pint of Gruel extra for Supper Daily.*

CLASS 3.

For Prisoners who have been in the Gaol more than One Month, and not more than Three Months, after Conviction :—

MALES

BREAKFAST,—8 ounces of Bread, and 1 pint of Oatmeal Gruel.

DINNER,
- Monday, Wednesday, and Friday, } 4 ounces of Bread, 12 ounces of Potatoes, and 8 ounces of Suet Pudding.
- Tuesday, Thursday, and Saturday, } 8 ounces of Bread, 8 ounces of Potatoes, and ¾ of a pint of Soup.
- Sunday, ... 10 ounces of Bread, and 2 ounces of Cheese.

SUPPER,—6 ounces of Bread, and 1 pint of Oatmeal Gruel.

FEMALES

BREAKFAST,—6 ounces of Bread, and 1 pint of Oatmeal Gruel.

DINNER,
- Monday, Wednesday, and Friday, } 4 ounces of Bread, 8 ounces of Potatoes, and 6 ounces of Suet Pudding.
- Tuesday, Thursday, and Saturday, } 6 ounces of Bread, 6 ounces of Potatoes, and ¾ of a pint of Soup.
- Sunday, ... 8 ounces of Bread, and 2 ounces of Cheese.

SUPPER,—6 ounces of Bread, and 1 pint of Oatmeal Gruel.

NOTE.—*When Prisoners of this Class are employed at hard Labour, Males and Females will have 1 ounce extra of Cheese on Sundays, and Males 3 ounces, and Females 2 ounces of Beef instead of Pudding on Mondays and Fridays.*

CLASS 4.

For Prisoners who have been in the Gaol more than Three Months, and not more than Six Months, after Conviction :—

MALES

BREAKFAST,—8 ounces of Bread, and 1 pint of Oatmeal Gruel.

DINNER,
- Monday, Wednesday, and Friday, } 4 ounces of Bread, 16 ounces of Potatoes, and 12 ounces of Suet Pudding.
- Tuesday, Thursday, and Saturday, } 8 ounces of Bread, 8 ounces of Potatoes, and 1 pint of Soup.
- Sunday, ... 10 ounces of Bread, and 3 ounces of Cheese.

SUPPER,—8 ounces of Bread, and 1 pint of Oatmeal Gruel.

FEMALES

BREAKFAST,—6 ounces of Bread, and 1 pint of Oatmeal Gruel.

DINNER,
- Monday, Wednesday, and Friday, } 4 ounces of Bread, 12 ounces of Potatoes, and 8 ounces of Suet Pudding.
- Tuesday, Thursday, and Saturday, } 6 ounces of Bread, 6 ounces of Potatoes, and 1 pint of Soup.
- Sunday, ... 8 ounces of Bread, and 2 ounces of Cheese.

SUPPER,—6 ounces of Bread, and 1 pint of Oatmeal Gruel.

NOTE.—*When Prisoners of this Class are employed at hard Labour, Males and Females will receive 1 ounce of Cheese extra on Sundays, and Males will receive 4 ounces, and Females 3 ounces of Meat instead of Pudding on Mondays and Fridays.*

CLASS 5.

For Prisoners who have been in the Gaol more than Six Months after Conviction :—

MALES

BREAKFAST,—8 ounces of Bread, and 1 pint of Oatmeal Gruel.

DINNER,
- Monday, Wednesday, and Friday, } 4 ounces of Bread, 16 ounces of Potatoes, and 12 ounces of Suet Pudding.
- Tuesday, Thursday, and Saturday, } 8 ounces of Bread, 16 ounces of Potatoes, and 1 pint of Soup.
- Sunday, ... 12 ounces of Bread, and 3 ounces of Cheese.

SUPPER,—8 ounces of Bread, and 1 pint of Oatmeal Gruel.

FEMALES

BREAKFAST,—6 ounces of Bread, and 1 pint of Oatmeal Gruel.

DINNER,
- Monday, Wednesday, and Friday, } 4 ounces of Bread, 12 ounces of Potatoes, and 8 ounces of Suet Pudding.
- Tuesday, Thursday, and Saturday, } 8 ounces of Bread, 12 ounces of Potatoes, and 1 pint of Soup.
- Sunday, ... 10 ounces of Bread, and 2 ounces of Cheese.

SUPPER,—6 ounces of Bread, and 1 pint of Oatmeal Gruel.

NOTE.—*When Prisoners of this Class are employed at hard Labour, Males and Females will receive 1 ounce of Cheese extra on Sundays, and Males will receive 4 ounces, and Females 3 ounces of Meat instead of Pudding on Mondays and Fridays.*

The Meat served instead of Pudding on Mondays and Fridays, in Classes 3, 4, and 5, to be weighed after cooking, and served cold.

Ingredient of Soup.—In every pint: The meat and liquor from 6 ounces of the necks, legs, and shins of Beef weighed with the bone previous to cooking, 1 ounce of Onions or Leeks, 1 ounce of Scotch Barley, 2 ounces of Carrots, Turnips, Parsnips, or other cheap vegetables, with Pepper and Salt; on Tuesdays and Saturdays the meat liquor of Mondays and Fridays to form part of the Soup.

The Soup on Tuesdays, Thursdays, and Saturdays, to contain 2 ounces of Split Peas in each pint, instead of 1 ounce of Barley.

Ingredients of Suet Pudding.—1¼ ounces of Suet, 3½ ounces of Flour, and about 8 ounces of Water to make 1 pound.

Ingredients of Indian-meal Pudding.—To consist of half-a-pint of skimmed Milk, to every 6 ounces of Meal.

Ingredients of Gruel.—To every pint, 2 ounces of coarse Scotch Oatmeal, with Salt.

Note.—The Gruel for Breakfast on Sundays in Class 4, and for Breakfast and Supper in Class 5, to contain 1 ounce of Molasses, per pint.

Prisoners sentenced by Court to solitary confinement, Males and Females, to be placed on the Progressive Scale of Diet, in accordance with the duration of their sentences.

Prisoners for examination before Trial, Misdemeanants of the first division who do not maintain themselves, destitute Debtors, and Prisoners committed by the County Courts, the diet of Class 3 without hard Labour, for any period not exceeding One calendar Month; that of Class 4, after the expiration of One Month, and till the completion of the Second calendar Month; and that of Class 5, if the detention should exceed Two calendar Months.

Debtors or Bankrupts committed by any Court of Law for fraud, or for any serious legal offence, and Deserters en route, the diet of Class 3.

Prisoners under punishment for prison offences under the provisions of the 42nd section of the Gaol Act, to have the diet of Class 1, for the first Seven Days; and after that to have 2 ounces extra of Bread per diem.

EASTER QUARTER SESSIONS, 1865.

C. J. TOTTENHAM, *Chairman.*
BREESE, *Clerk of the Peace.*

This Dietary having been submitted to me, I hereby certify the same as proper to be adopted in the Prison for the County of Merioneth.
WHITEHALL, 25th May, 1865. G. GREY.

OWEN REES, PRINTER AND STATIONER, BRIDGE STREET, DOLGELLEY.

Diet recommended for prisoners in Merioneth county gaol, 1865.
Merioneth Record Office ZQA/G/20.
By permission of Merioneth Record Office.

COUNTY OF DENBIGH.

RULES & REGULATIONS,

FOR THE

Government of the Gaol, and Female Prison,

AT RUTHIN,

MADE AT THE

General Quarter Sessions of the Peace, held at Denbigh, in and for the said County,

On Tuesday, 4th Day of April, in the year of our Lord, 1826,

And approved by the Honorable His Majesty's Judges of the Courts of Great Sessions for the several Counties of Chester, Flint, Denbigh, and Montgomery, on Saturday, 8th day of April, 1826.

RULES FOR CROWN PRISONERS.

I.
The bell shall ring at the opening and locking up of the rooms and cells, which shall be, from Lady-day to Michaelmas-day, at 6 o'clock in the morning, and 8 o'clock in the evening, and in the winter months, at 8 o'clock in the morning, and 8 in the evening ; and at all times the Prisoners shall be locked up in their day rooms before dusk in the evening.

II.
The wearing apparel of any Prisoner supposed to be in an impure and filthy state, shall be cleansed by order of the Keeper.

III.
No person shall be allowed admission into the prison, during the hour of prayer, the time of public worship, or before unlocking or after locking-up hours, and no person (except a Barrister or Solicitor) unless in the presence of the Keeper, or some person appointed by him ; and no person shall remain within the Prison after the hour of locking up, except in case of the sickness of a Prisoner, or some other cause assigned to the satisfaction of the Keeper.

IV.
Every Prisoner shall attend prayer and public worship, except in case of illness, or other reasonable cause to be allowed by the Keeper.

V.
Every Prisoner guilty of drunkenness, blasphemy, swearing, or any improper expression, or any abuse or disorderly conduct, shall be punished by close confinement at the discretion of the Keeper.

VI.
Every Prisoner shall make his or her own bed, and be washed before 9 o'clock every morning, on pain of forfeiting one day's allowance of provisions. Soap, towels, and combs provided for washing by the Gaoler.

VII.
No tobacco to be smoked except in the yards, on pain of forfeiting one day's allowance.

VIII.
No Prisoner shall take from another any money or other matter under the name of garnish, or under any other pretence. The chambers and cells shall be swept out by the Prisoners every morning before the same are left, and washed clean twice a week in the summer, and once in the winter.

IX.
The day rooms, stairs, and stair-cases shall be washed and cleansed by the Prisoners, on Mondays, Wednesdays, and Saturdays, in every week in the summer, and on Wednesdays and Saturdays in the winter ; and also the yards, baths, and privies in the same order.

X.
The Prisoners shall pump up as much water as will be required by the Keeper for the use of the Prisons.

XI.
The dust and other filth shall be laid in no other part than the common bins.

XII.
No Prisoner shall wantonly disturb another, nor sing, shout, or make a noise in the cells or any part of the Prisons, on pain of forfeiting one day's allowance.

XIII.
No wine, ale, beer, porter, or spirituous liquors of any kind shall be admitted under any pretence whatever, unless ordered by the Surgeon in his journal.

XIV.
No Prisoner shall spit on, soil, or abuse, or in any way disfigure any part of the Prisons, or waste or injure their bed or bedding, or any other furniture within the Prisons.

XV.
Every Prisoner shall at locking-up time present himself in the yard, and also at the door of the cell to the Turnkey.

XVI.
No gaming whatever shall be permitted on pain of forfeiting one day's allowance.

MOLD, PRINTED AT THE ALUN PRESS, BY E. AND J. LLOYD.

Rules for Crown prisoners in Ruthin gaol, 1826.
Denbighshire Record Office QSO/AG/1/83.
By permission of Denbighshire Record Office.

The Separate System: prisoners exercising in Pentonville prison, from Henry Mayhew, *The Criminal Prisons of London and scenes of Prison Life,* **1862.**

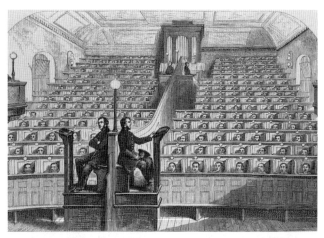

The Separate System: religious service in Pentonville prison from Henry Mayhew, *The Criminal Prisons of London and scenes of Prison Life,* **1862.**

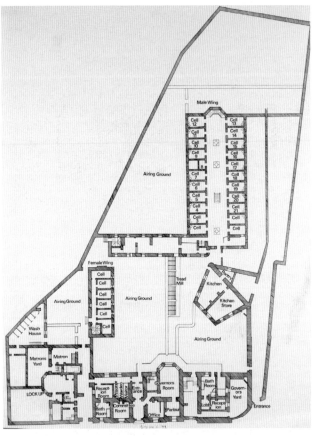

Modern version of a plan of Ruthin gaol originally drawn up in 1866.
Denbighshire Record Office QSO/AG/1/73.
By permission of Denbighshire Record Office.

Photograph inside Montgomery gaol, [late 19 cent.].
NLW Photo Album 918/001.

William Thomas, by continually assaulting him, starving him and refusing to provide him with necessary medicine could expect little sympathy. Sympathy was shown to those whom the crowd believed did not deserve to be hanged, and this could on occasions include those sentenced to death for murder. One such case was that of Cadwaladr Jones executed at Dolgellau, Merioneth, in 1877 for the murder of Sarah Hughes.

Cadwaladr Jones murdered Sarah Hughes by knocking her on the head with a stone on 4 June 1877and buried her near his house. Six weeks later when he heard that trained bloodhounds

were to be brought down from the north of England to search for her he panicked. He therefore dug up her body chopped it into sixteen pieces and threw them into the river in the belief that all the parts of the body would be washed out to sea, never to be seen again. Unfortunately for him parts of her body were found in the river. He could expect no sympathy for this shocking murder.

Public opinion, however, soon swung round in Cadwaladr Jones' favour. It appeared that Sarah Hughes was a woman of little if any morals. She had two illegitimate children and was expecting a third and it was claimed on the fateful night of her murder she had gone to see Jones to name him as the father of her unborn child, which would have ruined the life of this quiet, newly married young man. People began to believe that he had murdered her in a fit of rage and that he should be convicted of manslaughter not murder. Convicted of murder he was, and despite a petition pleading for his life to be spared the execution was ordered to go ahead. All the carpenters in the Dolgellau area refused to erect the gallows, and when Marwood the public executioner arrived in the town he was he was roundly hissed and booed by the people. Public support for Cadwaladr Jones was badly misplaced, however, since just before his execution he confessed that he did indeed murder Sarah Hughes in cold blood.

Photograph of Cadwaladr Jones hanged for the murder of Sarah Hughes in 1877
NLW Photo Album 1523.

Prisoners about to be executed were expected to 'die a good death' or 'to make a good end', that is, they were expected to confess their guilt, repent in the hope of forgiveness from the Lord, and go to meet their Maker in a state of grace. The prison chaplain and/or officiating minister put the prisoner under immense pressure to confess his guilt. Many of these confessions were published as ballads, booklets or in newspapers; they should not be taken at face value.

There is strong evidence to believe that the publishers themselves wrote many eighteenth century confessions, whilst newspaper editors or their staff composed those of the nineteenth century. In 1866 Robert Coe, who was hanged for the brutal murder of his 19 year old companion at Mountain Ash, Glamorgan, for the sake of £1-13-0 (£1-65) in 1865, made a full confession to the chaplain of Swansea prison. The confession was duly published in *The Cambria Daily Leader* or so it seemed. *The Swansea and Glamorgan Herald* reported a week later that:

'There is not one word of truth in the announcement - that an unwarrantable use has been made of the Chaplain's sacred name and office - in a word that the whole paragraph from beginning to end is a vile fabrication, a bare-faced falsehood...'

The response of the prison chaplain is on the following page.

William Griffith, executed in Anglesey for the attempted murder of his wife, was one of many who simply refused to 'die a good death'. A disapproving journalist from the *North Wales Chronicle* described how

On the morning of execution, having been for a few minutes left alone, he tore up the wooden bench on which his bed was placed, and fixing it against the door, for some time prevented all access from without. The door being at length forced, he was secured; and every effort which humanity and Christian feeling could suggest, having been in vain used to compose his mind, the requisite preparations were made for carrying the sentence of the law into execution, the criminal all the while uttering the most agonizing cries and groans.

A little before ten o'clock Samuel Burrows, the Chester executioner, was admitted into the cell and, after a desperate struggle succeeded in pinioning the prisoner with a cord at the elbows. The Rev. Chaplain then commenced reading the funeral service, and the prisoner was led, or rather dragged, between two officers to the scaffold, on which the javelin men and others whose duty required their presence, were already placed. When arrived at the scaffold and placed under the beam, Griffith, who appears to have reserved his strength for a last struggle, made a desperate resistance to the executioner putting the halter round his neck, and even when this was accomplished, he made continual efforts to displace it till the drop was withdrawn, which was done within five minutes from the time he came upon the scaffold. His death was to all appearance instantaneous, and after hanging for about an hour his body was cut down and placed in a coffin for interment, which took place in the evening.

The day after his condemnation, Griffith had an interview with his wife, but without expressing any remorse for the dreadful crime he had attempted against her. Indeed, he subsequently expressed himself as hardly dealt with in being to have his life taken away, while his intended victim had escaped the effects of his brutal attempt.

The personal appearance of the prisoner was very unprepossessing. His countenance bore every mark of ferocity, with which his clumsy but strongly knit frame was completely in accordance.

The melancholy fate of this unhappy man presents a frightful picture of the close of an irreligious and immoral life, by a violent and ignominous death, and we sincerely hope will operate as an awful warning to those who are weak enough to deceive themselves into the damning belief that it is an easy thing at the last hour to obtain that grace which they despise in the course of their life. Even on a sick bed the death of such must present a frightful scene,—on a scaffold it is awful past description.

An immense multitude was present at the execution, and even after it was over, crowds continued to throng into Beaumaris, the general impression throughout the neighbouring country being that the sentence would not be executed before twelve o'clock.

We must not omit to notice that the utmost humanity and kindness was shewn to the unhappy man, during the whole time of his confinement, by the undersheriff and bailiff, and by the jailor and his wife, Mr. and Mrs. Jones, whose attention to his wants and comforts reflects the highest honour on their humanity.

It is upwards of forty years since an execution took place before in Beaumaris, a circumstance highly honourable to the population of Anglesey, and we sincerely hope that generations will pass without witnessing another.

The North Wales Chronicle's report on William Griffith's execution at Beaumaris, 16 Sept. 1830

The chaplain of Swansea gaol's letter to *The Cambrian* denying that the confession of Robert Coe published in *The Cambria Daily Leader*, 6 April 1866, was genuine.

'all possible means for his conversion were unceasingly used by the chaplain to the [Beaumaris] gaol and several individuals who took a pious interest in his spiritual welfare, we are truly sorry to say that he died as he lived, without any manifestation of Christian feeling.'

Not everyone went quietly to the scaffold. Some pretended to care little for their eventual fate; others joked with the crowd or waved to friends, whilst others such as William Griffith were defiant to the end, resisting the hangman and officers at his execution.

These were attempts at bravado; attempts to come to terms with the awful fate awaiting them. The reality of executions was very different from that portrayed in ballads and newspapers. Most went to the scaffold in a state of utter terror. Often the man who put on a show of bravery on his way to the scaffold was drunk out of his mind. Most went to the scaffold trembling with fear, praying or crying continually, and had to be helped to the scaffold. Many were on the verge of insanity. William Morris, one of the Glanareth murderers, fell into a fit and was totally senseless when he came to the gallows and to be held up whilst the rope was placed round his neck. A pirate hanged in 1865 had to be hanged seated from a chair. Few ballads recounted the countless men and women who died having urinated or excreted in their clothes.

CAN NEWYDD,

Yn rhoi Hanes cyflawn am

Gyffesiad Dafydd Evans,

Am Lofruddiaeth ei Gariad,

HANNAH DAVIES,

Yr hon a gyflawnodd ar nos Sadwrn, Mehefin 13, 1829, ar Fynydd Pencareg, ac am ba un ei dienyddiwyd yn Nghaerfyrddin, ar yr 21 o Fedi canlynol.—Wedi esgyn o hono y tro cyntaf i'r grogbren, syrthiodd rhyw bethau perthynol iddi, a chwympodd i lawr, pryd y gwridiodd ei wyneb, ac yr haerai yn ddifrifddwys, *nad oedd crogi ddwywaith am yr un trosedd;* eithr bu gorfod arno ail-esgyn i'r pren dyoddef, ac yn fuan trosglwyddwyd ef i dragywyddoldeb.

Gan STEPHEN JONES, Llanfaeryw.

CYD-NESWCH yma i wrando, bob Cymro'n ddi nacâd,
Cewch glywed fel mae llygredd pur ryfedd mewn parâd;
Mae'r hanes yn alarus ac anghysurus iawn,
Er hyn gall fod yn rhybudd, modd ufudd, ddedwydd ddawn.

Ballad entitled in translation *A New Song giving a full Account of David Evans' Confession* with a note about the failure of the first attempt to hang him, 1829.

Convicts were strangled not hanged and death was certainly not instantaneous. Kicking their legs many chocked over minutes. Lord Ferrers took about four minutes to die when he was hanged in 1760. The new method of hanging-the-drop-made no difference. Thomas Thomas, hanged in Brecon in 1845, took two minutes to die whilst James Griffiths, aged 18, also hanged in Brecon, took four minutes to die in 1859. David Roberts, hanged in 1888 for the murder of a Cowbridge drover, 'did not die easily. He continued to show signs of life for some minutes.' Little wonder then that relatives and friends of those sentenced to death, especially those convicted of theft, tried to shorten their agony by beating the prisoner on the chest or pulling his legs downwards.

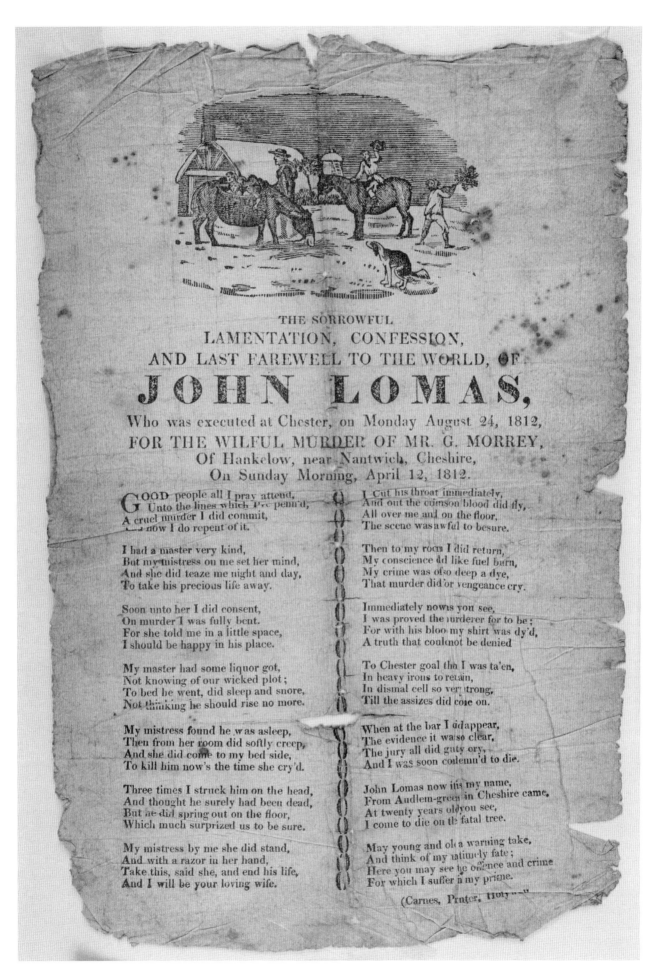

THE SORROWFUL
LAMENTATION, CONFESSION,
AND LAST FAREWELL TO THE WORLD, OF

JOHN LOMAS,

Who was executed at Chester, on Monday August 24, 1812,
FOR THE WILFUL MURDER OF MR. G. MORREY,
Of Hankelow, near Nantwich, Cheshire,
On Sunday Morning, April 12, 1812.

GOOD people all I pray attend,
Unto the lines which I've penn'd,
A cruel murder I did commit,
And now I do repent of it.

I had a master very kind,
But my mistress on me set her mind,
And she did teaze me night and day,
To take his precious life away.

Soon unto her I did consent,
On murder I was fully bent.
For she told me in a little space,
I should be happy in his place.

My master had some liquor got,
Not knowing of our wicked plot;
To bed he went, did sleep and snore,
Not thinking he should rise no more.

My mistress found he was asleep,
Then from her room did softly creep,
And she did come to my bed side,
To kill him now's the time she cry'd.

Three times I struck him on the head,
And thought he surely had been dead,
But he did spring out on the floor,
Which much surprized us to be sure.

My mistress by me she did stand,
And with a razor in her hand,
Take this, said she, and end his life,
And I will be your loving wife.

I cut his throat immediately,
And out the crimson blood did fly,
All over me and on the floor,
The scene was awful to besure.

Then to my room I did return,
My conscience did like fuel burn,
My crime was of so deep a dye,
That murder did for vengeance cry.

Immediately now as you see,
I was proved the murderer for to be;
For with his blood my shirt was dy'd,
A truth that could not be denied

To Chester goal then I was ta'en,
In heavy irons to retain,
In dismal cell so very strong,
Till the assizes did come on.

When at the bar I did appear,
The evidence it was so clear,
The jury all did guilty cry,
And I was soon condemn'd to die.

John Lomas now is my name,
From Audlem-green in Cheshire came,
At twenty years old you see,
I come to die on the fatal tree.

May young and old a warning take,
And think of my untimely fate;
Here you may see the offence and crime
For which I suffer in my prime.

(Carnes, Printer, Holy——

A true confession?

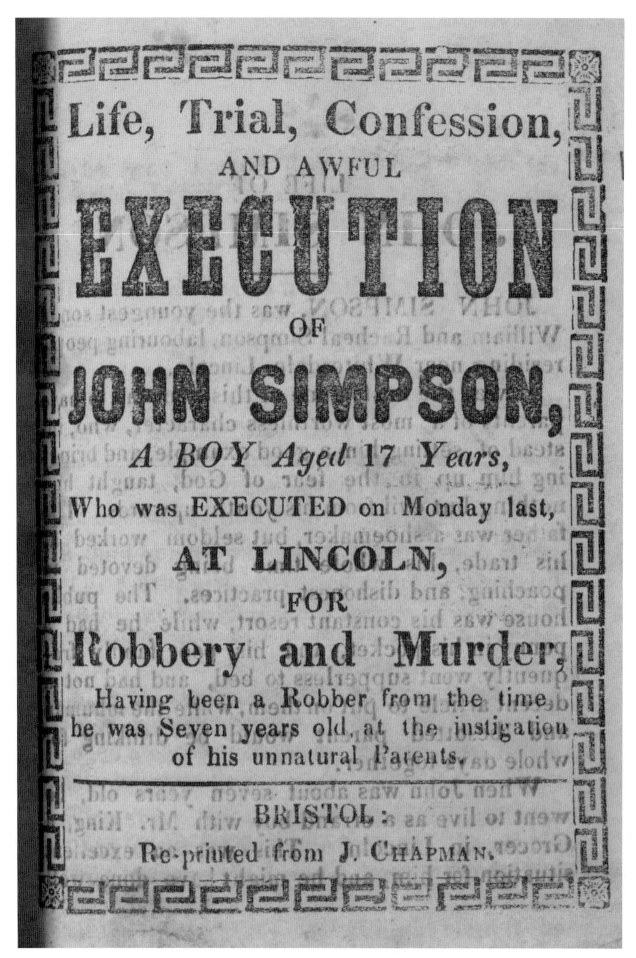

Life, Trial, Confession,

AND AWFUL

EXECUTION

OF

JOHN SIMPSON,

A BOY Aged 17 Years,

Who was EXECUTED on Monday last,

AT LINCOLN,

FOR

Robbery and Murder,

Having been a Robber from the time he was Seven years old, at the instigation of his unnatural Parents.

BRISTOL:

Re-printed from J. CHAPMAN.

A true confession?

Hangmen could not be depended upon to carry out a clean, swift execution. Sometimes the rope broke or the cross beam fell loose, as happened when David Evans was executed at Carmarthen in 1829. He dropped to the ground like a ball out of a cannon according to one newspaper. Evans claimed his freedom in the mistaken belief - widely shared at the time - that a man could not be hanged twice. He was badly mistaken. He was promptly picked up, repositioned and hanged to cries of 'Shame. Let him go.' according to one newspaper.

Executioners misjudged the length of the drop required to affect a quick death. When the hangman tried to execute Robert Johnson in Edinburgh in 1818 the drop was too short so that his toes were still touching the ground half standing, half suspended. One of the common failings of hangmen was that they measured the condemned's height and not his weight. For decades men and women dropped inches to kick their way to death on the end of short ropes. When longer ones were used the condemned's head was often jerked apart from his body. Apart from their lack of technical expertise, hangmen were often drunk at executions. Lewis Francis, a part-time hangman in Glamorgan at the end of the eighteenth century, was described as 'a drunk, thief and beggar.'

Last minute reprieves were rare. An unusual example is the case of a Ceredigion pair who were tramping their way to London with their baby girl in 1834. They were charged at Worcester with the murder of a local gentleman who had given them a bill of exchange (similar to a modern cheque) drawn in his name to pay for food and lodging. The gentleman was found dead that same evening. The couple were convicted of murder and sentenced to hang. On the scaffold the mother in tears begged the watching crowd to look after her baby. Suddenly, burdened with guilt that two innocent people were about to be hanged, the real murderer confessed and the pair were reprieved.

The law prescribed worse punishments than hanging. In cases of treason, the condemned was drawn on a hurdle, hanged, cut down whilst still alive, disembowelled and castrated, beheaded and quartered. Women were not subject to this kind of mutilation but for petty treason (killing her husband or master/mistress) the punishment was burning at the stake. This was the fate that befell a maidservant who murdered her master. Humphrey Jenkins. He was seen by his two maids and head servant counting out £40. They poisoned his drink, locked him in a room where he eventually died. Foul play was not suspected until the two maids quarrelled over the division of the spoils, the head servant having already fled. The younger maid turned King's evidence to save herself, the elder maid was tried at Brecon and sentenced to be to be hanged until half dead and then burnt at the stake. According to a balled published in 1772 she was tied to the stake and burnt with tar and faggots. It is more likely, however, that she was dead before being burned, because it was widely believed in the eighteenth century that executioners strangled women with a cord before lighting the fire. It was also believed that executioners allowed men to die on the gallows before disembowelling and castrating them.

Even after execution the history of the condemned man's body was still far from over. As an example to others, the bodies of those hanged could be ordered to be left on gibbets, often where the offence took place, to rot and stench. Gibbeting, by which is meant suspending a dead body in a metal frame, was meant to serve as a warning and an example. Working people had a great horror of hanging in chains for the shame it brought the family. Neighbours were none too pleased either. Family shame, no doubt, was the reason why Mary Thomas was charged with cutting down a gibbet on which her husband had been hung for a robbery in 1777.

After the passing of the Murder Act in 1752 the corpses of a hanged man or woman could be handed over to the surgeons to 'dissect or anatomise', in other words to carry out experiments. People feared being anatomised and there is no doubt that it caused deep resentment and anguish as the frantic attempts by friends and family of the dead to prevent this happening prove. Being handed over to the surgeons brought added shame and disgrace upon families. It was regarded as more terrible than death and was perhaps the greatest indignity that might befall a condemned man.

Ballad entitled in translation *A New Song about a Husband and Wife from Wales Sentenced to Death for a Murder Committed By Another together with an Account of the Execution of the Murderer.*

³²/₂ LLOFRUDDIAETH.

NEU,

GAN

Yn dangos,

MARWOLAETH

Mr. Humphry Jenkins,

Yr hwn a laddwyd rhwng ei Was a'i ddwy Forwyn.

Yn rhoddi gwir ac union Hanes o'r Modd y llofgwyd un o'r Morwynion wrth Aber-honddu, y trydydd dydd o fis Mai. A'r Gwas y ddiangodd ymaith o'r Wlad.

Gwneuthuriad PHILYB THOMAS.

CAERFYRDDIN,

Argraffwyd dros Efan Wiliam gan I. Rofs.

M,DCC,LXXII.

28.
Rhoi 'r Judge y ferdiƈt iddi grogi,
Yn hanner marw cyn ei llofgi,
Fel gallai eraill gym'ryd rhybydd,
Wrth weithred hon a'i throm ddihenydd.

29.
A'r trydydd Dydd o Fai diwedda,
Y rhoed hi dan y pren dioddedofa,
Mewn pig a llyfg hi gadd ei llofgi,
Yn ulw mân wrth Aberhonddu.

30.
A'r gwas a ffodd o'r wlad yn fuan,
Pan Ddatguddiwyd y drwg allan,
Ni wyr un Dyn p'le gwnaeth ei drigfa,
Gwedi ddilyn ffaelu ei ddala.

31.
Aed i Loegr aed i Werddon,
Fyth ni ddiange rhag trallodion,
Cerdded dir a Dwr ile gallo,
Mae gwaed ei feiftr gwirion arno.

32.
Fe ddichon pob darllenydd gofio,
Fod gwaed Abel etto 'n crio,
Er dechreu'r Byd mae Duw 'n cyhoeddi
Pob dirgel Lanas i oleuni.

33.
Mae 'r ferythur Lan yn roi rhybuddion
I wach'lyd tywallt gwaed y gwirion,
A'r dyn a'i gwnel mae 'n byw mewn gofal
Nes del digofaint Duw a dial.

34.
Gwaith Duw fydd yn rhoddi oes a bywyd
A chennad Duw yw'r angeu i'n fymmud,
Cymmeryd gallu Duw o'i ddwylo,
Wnaeth llawer myrdd o'rrhai fy'n mwrddr

P. Thomas.   35. Ma

Part of a ballad entitled in translation *Murder or a Song giving an account of the death of Mr Humphrey Jenkins who was killed by his Servant and two Maids* **describing how a servant maid was burnt at the stake for murdering her master. The ballad was published or reprinted in 1772, the murder occurred around 1700.**

Further reading.

Christopher Culpin, *Crime and Punishment Through Time* (Collins Educational, 1997).

Dewi Davies, *Law and Disorder in Breconshire 1750-1880* (D. G. &A. S. Evans, Brecon, 1991).

V. A. C. Gatrel, *The hanging tree: execution and the English people, 1770-1868* (Oxford University Press, 1994).

Robert Hughes, *The Fatal Shore* (Pan Books, 1988).

David J.V. Jones, *Crime in Nineteenth-Century Wales* (University of Wales Press, 1992).

Henry Mayhew, *The criminal prisons of London, and scenes of prison life* (Griffin, Bohn and Company, 1862).

Keith Owen, *Crime and punishment* (Longman and University of Wales Press, 1992).